God
Among Us

God Among Us

Glimpses of Glory in the Baja

The adventure began with Charla Pereau's true story of faith in the book, Charla's Children. *Twenty years later, God continues to reveal Himself in powerful and personal ways through this amazing work in Baja, Mexico.*

Linda Baker Kaahanui

Sovereign World

Sovereign World Ltd
PO Box 777
Tonbridge
Kent TN11 0ZS
England

ISBN 1 85240 380 2

Cover design by CCD, www.ccdgroup.co.uk
Typeset by CRB Associates, Reepham, Norfolk
Printed in the United States of America

Contents

A Personal Note from Charla

It has been more than four decades since Chuck and I cradled a two-day-old Zapotec Indian baby in our arms and wondered why the God of the universe had sent us this precious gift. Perhaps his life was being spared from the tyranny of poverty. Could it be that we were chosen to raise Mexico's Billy Graham?

When Charles Curtis was six years old, we made our first trip south of the border, never to be the same again. The little ones we saw – beggars, those with shoe shine boxes, and children foraging through the garbage dump in hopes of finding their daily bread – they all looked like our precious son at home. God, the Holy Spirit, filled our hearts with loving compassion for the least of these.

Charles Curtis is now married and works for Gelson's Markets. He and his wife Lisa, have five beautiful children. They are a loving Christian family. Through a supernatural experience, Curtis' natural mother from Oaxaca was brought back into our lives. That story will be told in a personal sequel to *Charla's Children*.

In 1966 we made our unforgettable trip to the then remote desert of the Baja Peninsula. There, in the dark of night, we came upon some old uninhabited adobe ruins. We heard the voices of little children where there were no children. God gave us a vision of a home for children, a great harvest of souls for the kingdom of God, and a Bible institute like the one I attended as a young woman.

It was at Bible school that Jesus, my Savior, became the Lord of my life and gave me a passion to reach the lost. Heaven and hell became real to me and I recognized that the decisions we make here and now determine our eternal destiny.

The ministry in Mexico has expanded beyond all expectation. The book, *Charla's Children*, was published by Bethany House in 1981 and was revised, updated, and self-published in 1987. To everyone's amazement, it was awarded the coveted Angel Award. That self-published book is still in demand and we have received countless reports from readers of changed lives.

Prayer has always been the foundation, the center, and the power of this ministry. Staff and visitors meet each morning to worship God, ask for His guidance for the work of the ministry, and draw from His grace. We pray for God to send forth the laborers and He does so. Volunteers from around the world have come and given their best to the service of The Master. They are the "Who's Who" in the kingdom of God. Intercessors across the nations have faithfully prayed for Chuck and me and our co-workers. Their prayers have carried us through the dry valleys to the tops of the mountains and to the other side of the storms at sea.

We have learned to trust in Jesus. We have learned to depend upon His word. If we had never had problems, we wouldn't know how wonderfully He could solve them. We wouldn't know what faith in God can do!

We press on!

Charla

Introduction

Charla's Children told the beginning of a remarkable story. Twenty years have passed since the writing of that book and the story continues to unfold.

Corrine Ehrick, who served at the mission in Vicente Guerrero for nine years, tells of the day she asked Charla to pray for a new room to live in. Her current quarters were far from any bathroom and had rat-infested walls. She listened in surprise as Charla did not pray for a room; she prayed for a house! A week later, a couple traveling down the Baja highway donated a beautiful motor home. As Corrine moved in, she realized she had learned a lesson. "Charla's God was bigger than mine!"

Through the pages of *Charla's Children*, many of us followed Charla's journey and watched her grow in faith. We saw how God delights in going beyond the limits we place upon Him, bursting the boundaries of our little expectations. So often those expectations are not based upon who He is, but upon our own small understanding of His love and of His willingness to demonstrate that love in powerful, supernatural ways. May this book continue to expand your vision of who He is!

This book compiles many more stories of God at work, using ordinary people to accomplish what no one thought possible. Out of failures, out of weakness, out of laughably meager resources, the miracle of dependence emerges, proving God is utterly dependable!

As you meet the people involved, you will see stories of redemption, enacted again and again. Lives once ruined and discarded are touched and reborn by the power of God's Spirit. For anyone who feels overwhelmed by failure or problems that seem hopeless, take heart! Here is proof that Jesus is indeed the great Redeemer. No sin is so great that Jesus' blood cannot wash away every stain of guilt. No life is so mangled or in a pit so deep that Jesus cannot pull it up from the depths and make it utterly new.

You will find stories of majestic sovereignty. No human plans or programs could have so perfectly brought together all the pieces of this ministry. No human ingenuity or will power could have overcome the obstacles that stood in the way.

For anyone who has a desire to serve the King but is discouraged by a lack of talent, resources, or experience, take courage! Here is proof that your God is bigger than any lack. He seeks only those who are willing to obey – willing to love others more than self, willing to trust the truth of His words, *"For whoever wants to save his life will lose it, but whoever loses his life for me and for the gospel will save it"* (Mark 8:35).

Perhaps your experience of God has been limited by distance – that invisible gulf between the tangible and the spiritual realms. Has your heart ever desperately longed to leap across that chasm, rip away the veil of heaven, and make direct contact with the Living God? You're normal! God has placed a natural yearning in all mankind, *"... so that men would seek him and perhaps reach out for him and find him"* it says in Acts 17:27. That same verse ends in a wonderful truth – *"... though he is not far from each one of us."* May God use this book to help tear the veil. He is personally involved, actively involved, passionately involved with people. He wants you to know how very near He is to you!

Many people at Foundation for His Ministry (FFHM) have shared their stories and experiences to make this book possible. Sometimes the telling was exciting, sometimes it was painful and embarrassing. Always, the stories were told for your sake, dear reader. Through this book, may God's love and His power at work in His people become a reality that brings great hope, encouragement and inspiration to your life!

Prologue

In 1961, Chuck and Charla Pereau lived lives typical of most church-going Christians in America. They were busy raising three children while Chuck worked as a Los Angeles City fireman and Charla supervised the Sunday School Department at Emmanuel Lutheran Church. They gave to missions as God led and one day sent $10.00 to a Lutheran missionary in Oaxaca, Mexico. Life changed forever when the receipt came – along with a request that they adopt a yet-to-be-born Zapotec Indian baby. Charla recalls, "It was the weirdest letter I'd ever read. I send a little money and they want to send me a free sample!" Charla adamantly refused, arguing that the last thing she needed was another baby in their already crowded, small house. But arguing with God proved futile and, four months later, she was flying back from Texas with a little pink bundle in her arms. The entire family instantly fell in love with the new arrival, Charles Curtis. As Chuck put it later, "God now had a hook in our jaw."

Five years later, Charla visited an orphanage in the border city of Tijuana, Mexico. As she looked around at the dim, dirty rooms, the poor food and children in rags, her heart broke. In each dark, brown-eyed face, she saw the reflection of her own little boy back home. It was horrible to imagine him in this place and how easily it could have been like this for him. It shocked her that such poverty could exist right at the doorstep of the wealthiest country on earth. As Charla wept for these children, she knew she could never again ignore the need God had put before her.

Shortly after this whisper from God, the Pereaus were miraculously led to a cluster of abandoned buildings 180 miles south of the border in Colonia Vicente Guerrero, on the Baja peninsula. Through visions, a remarkable outpouring of the Holy Spirit on the eleven orphans they found there, divine provision and countless miracles, Foundation for His Ministry (FFHM) was born.

It began simply: a North Hollywood housewife making a seventeen-hour drive each month on bone-jarring, pot-holed dirt roads to deliver whatever food, clothing, powdered milk and blankets she could collect to a group of kids she had met out in the middle of the Baja desert. When friends could help, they did. When Chuck could come with her, he did. Eventually, the supply runs became a weekly trek for Chuck, who took advantage of his three-day leaves from the fire department.

A prayer group of ten of the Pereau's closest friends met each Friday night for worship and intercessory prayer. That group became the board for FFHM. Forty years later, that group (including five of the original members) still meets each week to seek God's continuous guidance.

Without this commitment to prayer, the Foundation might never have listened when God said to buy 72 acres of land in the middle of the desert, an unpromising expanse of dust and wild brush. Even friends liked to tease Charla, asking, "Who do you plan to preach to, the cactus?" As it turned out, an underground river was discovered thirteen years after the purchase and the entire, surrounding San Quintin valley began to boom with agricultural development.

The sparsely populated area needed field laborers to handle the harvests. In 1978, U.S. corporations and Mexican ranchers started a migration by bringing 1,000 workers up from the state of Oaxaca. Each year, the numbers increased. In 1990, 50,000 laborers arrived in one year alone. These workers came from indigenous Indian groups that lived in the jungled mountains of Mexico's southern tip. They came on the promise of work. No one told them they would be paid only half what a Mexican would make, that there was no housing, no sanitation, no medical care, no school for their children. They have continued to come by the thousands – only to find themselves in a trap of inescapable poverty. When they discover the subhuman conditions, many save their meager funds and go home, never to return to Baja. For many others, saving the bus fare proves impossible. Now, instead of deserted wasteland, the Foundation's mission is surrounded by miles and miles of cultivated fields and dozens of migrant worker camps – fields white for the harvest, both literally and spiritually.

In 1982, two events dramatically changed the work and character of the mission.

The first change came via the state of Florida. Florida's agricultural lobby felt threatened by the volume of tomatoes now being grown in the Baja Peninsula for export into the U.S. They could not compete with the prices, so a law was passed that tomatoes coming from Mexico had to be $2\frac{1}{2}$ inches in diameter. There was no way of communicating this new regulation to the growers of Baja and Sinaloa. The tomato harvest was great. Every vehicle that could be drafted into service was loaded to the brink and headed north. When they got to the U.S. border agricultural inspection area, the drivers were confounded when the inspector took out a ruler or a scale to measure the diameter of the tomatoes. 90% of the crop did not meet the $2\frac{1}{2}$ inch diameter criteria. The trucks were turned around and sent back. Mountains of vine ripened tomatoes could be seen rotting along the roads heading south.

The ranchers had made great investments in irrigation systems and truckloads of stakes used to tie up the plants had been brought into the Baja Peninsula. This devastating loss meant they could not pay their workers. Hundreds of destitute families came to the mission seeking food, cardboard to build shelter, blankets, and clothing. They had been uprooted from their homes in Oaxaca and arrived on a one-way ticket. Now they had no money and no way to return home. With this crisis, the mission made a fundamental shift from being a simple home for needy children to a center of mercy ministry to the entire San Quintin Valley, especially the migrant workers living in the camps.

The second change came that same year when a 15-year-old Triqui boy from Oaxaca was found, left for dead, at the beach. Lucio had been shot in the head. He was taken to El Buen Pastor hospital in San Quintin. Through medical intervention, his life was saved, but he was blind. There was no help for a blind Indian boy in the region, so Lucio was sent to the mission in Vicente Guerrero. Pastor David Mendez took Lucio in and he was given the job of cleaning the chapel with a push broom.

The children were drawn to this kind, blind boy. They loved Lucio and prayed God would restore his sight. In concert, they proclaimed that a boy named Lucio, which means light, should not be walking in darkness. They continued to pray for him. The unforgettable day came when the children ran into the orphanage building crying, "Lucio can see!" They saw him sweeping the refuse onto a dustpan. There was no explanation. Lucio's declaration was simply, "I was blind and now I see."

Word spread and suddenly the small chapel, used by the children and staff, could not hold the crowds coming in from miles around. Meetings moved to the old, historic cinema building and a thriving, community-based church was born. That church has since established ten satellite churches in surrounding areas.

With these two events, the mission grew into a ministry far beyond anything Chuck and Charla had ever asked or imagined. What has happened in the last twenty years? God has revealed Himself in ever-increasing and glorious ways.

George Müller once said that his most important activity was to glorify God by demonstrating the reality of One who is still answering prayer and who is still intervening in our lives and is active today. Stories were chosen for this book for this very same reason. They show us what God is like, the nature of His heart. You may not live in Mexico or on a mission field, but God is the same in every place, in every moment. May you find in these stories a fresh revelation of His faithfulness, the nearness of His presence and the kindness of His ways.

PART I

Our Redeeming God

After the terrorist attacks on the World Trade Center and the Pentagon on September 11, 2001, we saw an incredible display of selfless courage as rescue workers did everything in their power to save others. Through the years we have seen international aid workers arrive at every type of disaster zone, whether it was famine, flood, earthquake or war. In the midst of the suffering, someone always asks, "Where is God?"

God is on the greatest search and rescue mission of all. He does not see just the catastrophes that make world headlines. He sees the personal heartaches, the silent tears. And He has sent the ultimate Rescuer into this world to do everything possible, everything necessary, to save us.

Everywhere, God sees mankind mired in the misery of his own sin, suffering from the sins of others, and trapped by the power of that sin. Where is God? God is here, on the scene, with His hands stretched out and nailed to the beams of a cross, stretched out to save.

Jesus expressed His own mission statement best when He read from the prophet Isaiah:

> *"The Spirit of the Sovereign* Lord *is on me,*
> *because the* Lord *has anointed me*
> *to preach good news to the poor.*
> *He has sent me to bind up the broken-hearted,*
> *to proclaim freedom for the captives*
> *and release from darkness for the prisoners . . . "*

(Isaiah 61:1)

When Chuck and Charla first came to Vicente Guerrero, a little boy who had never read the Bible uttered these same words under the anointing of the Holy Spirit. His prophetic words made it clear; Jesus is still on a mission!

In Part I, you will meet some of those whose lives tell the story of our redeeming God. He is truly One who reaches into the darkest shadows, the lowest pits, and calls out those whom the world would consider of no value or promise. To Jesus they are precious. They are the very reason for His rescue mission, the object of His great love.

Chapter 1

Led Home

"Some wandered in desert wastelands,
  finding no way to a city where they could settle.
They were hungry and thirsty,
  and their lives ebbed away.
Then they cried out to the LORD in their trouble,
  and he delivered them from their distress.
He led them by a straight way
  to a city where they could settle.
Let them give thanks to the LORD for his unfailing love
  and his wonderful deeds for men,
for he satisfies the thirsty
  and fills the hungry with good things."
                    (Psalm 107:4–9)

Somehow, the axe slipped and Raul lost his balance. His arm shot out just in time to catch the sharp edge of the falling blade. Blood poured from the deep gash. Shocked, the little boy stared at the exposed bones of his left hand, too stunned to cry. But a moment later, searing pain erupted in a torrent of tears and wails. Cradling his limp arm in the blood-soaked tails of his ragged shirt, Raul staggered toward the house.

Light from propane lamps gleamed in the window and Raul could hear the jumbled voices of a family at dinner. He felt . . . so . . . dizzy. Every heartbeat sent another surge of agony through his frail, underfed body. He was almost there . . . almost. He stumbled on the doorstep, landing his shoulder against the barred, rough wood with a weak thud. "Help me," he thought, but no words came. Just a wave of blackness.

The door opened, pulling away Raul's support. Instinctively, he jerked to catch himself and screamed with new pain.

Dark eyes glared down at him and voices called from behind the towering form of his boss.

"Who is it, Papa?" a voice whined.

"Is that the shepherd boy? Tell him not to bother us at dinner."

Raul could barely whimper. "Please, senor . . . "

"You really are a stupid boy, aren't you? And careless too. Look what you've done now." The rancher's deep, irritated voice cut through Raul's blurred thoughts. He saw the big hand on the door twitch with indecision. Help this dirty, indigent barnrat of a child? No, he was only deciding whether or not to slam the door.

Now a sharp, female voice called out. "Tell him we need that wood. He'd better not be expecting food unless he goes back and gets it. I'm not feeding him for nothing."

Raul bit back tears, the pain in his heart almost more unbearable than the torture of his cleft hand. He wasn't going to cry, not here. Not in front of these snobs. Snobs and liars, that's what they were.

Abandoned at age three, Raul had been left with his grandmother. At age five, when his grandmother decided she could not afford to feed an extra mouth, he had been given to a widow with no children. For two years, she kept him like a trained animal, a beast to do chores for scraps of food.

One day a stranger came through the village, noticed Raul's sorry circumstances, and offered him a job and a home. Raul ran off with this man, but the home he provided turned out to be no more than a patch of straw with the animals. The man had a proud family of his own that refused to be shamed by the addition of a dark-skinned Oaxacan Indian boy.

Raul's life became an endless stretch of lonely days in the hills. Each dawn, the wife would hand him a small pouch of food that never lasted beyond his morning hunger pangs. He spent the sunlight hours in the company of sheep and cows. He spent his nights in the barn, awash in the pungent smell of dung and musky hides. It was a life without friends, without family and without hope.

That night, Raul nursed his own mangled hand. Using his teeth and one good hand, he pulled and knotted an old rag around the gash. Curling into the straw, Raul fell asleep, aching for the mother he couldn't remember.

The afternoon sun blazed over shimmering hills, pressing its heat into every crack of the arroyo floor. The banks of a vanished river gaped open, the clay split and hard like Raul's own chapped lips.

"Hey, little Indio!" A boy several years older suddenly appeared, along with two others. "How long are you gonna live with animals?" He pointed to a skinny cow. "Is that your mom?"

"You shouldn't let them treat you like that." A second boy shook his head and pointed to the scars on Raul's legs. "My uncle's a drunk and he doesn't even beat our dog like that."

Raul ran his shepherd's stick over the scabs on his leg that itched because they never healed. "I'm OK." He glanced nervously at the goat in the brush. Did they plan to steal from him?

"Well, I know one thing for sure," the skinniest boy chimed in. "No one's ever gonna beat me again." He raised his shirt just enough for Raul to see the red, swollen welt across his ribs. "Tomorrow, we're outta here."

"Yahoo!" The other boys hooted. "Mexico City! Forget this place. We're gonna get rich!"

"Hey, goatboy, you should come too."

They left, but Raul could hear their laughter and voices boasting of grandiose dreams long after the heat waves had liquefied their forms. "That's it," he determined. "I'm nine years old. Old enough to decide for myself. I'm not going to do this anymore." Something else they said ... Mexico City ... pricked his imagination. Vaguely, he remembered an aunt had once told him his mother was in Mexico City. He would find her! Other children had parents. He had seen them in the village. Mothers holding babies, buying sticks of candy for little boys, laughing and fussing over their children with loving care. Why shouldn't he have a mother?

The stars were bright that night. Raul slept outside, tossing restlessly on a flea-infested saddle blanket. The celestial expanse made him feel very small. Sometimes he wondered about God. Did He exist? If He did, didn't He see Raul? Or was Raul too small?

That night, Raul had a dream. A man stood before him, dressed in white with a golden belt. He stretched his arms out to Raul, motioning him to come. Raul had never seen Him before nor heard of anyone like Him. Something deep inside him recognized the man only as a superior being. He thought, "I know this man, yet I don't know who He is." Drawn by a strange sense of comfort, Raul ran to Him and kissed His feet.

A week later, Raul found two of the boys who still talked of running away. That night they waited by the road, at a bend where the potholes forced cargo trucks to slow to a crawl and where the outcropping rocks were big enough to hide three stowaways.

The truck ride from Oaxaca to Mexico City took all night. Choking clouds of exhaust and dust finally woke Raul from his sleep. The truck had pulled into a busy terminal and marketplace. This was it! Raul climbed, then tumbled over the high tailgate before the truck came to its final stop, landing on a heap of sacked oranges.

"Hey! You! You're gonna pay for those!"

A stick descended from the glare of blinding sunlight. Raul's arm went up, deflecting the blow, just as he scuttled back under the belly of the truck. Dense masses of people swarmed by, their heads cut off from view by the overhanging truckbed. Where did they all come from? Raul stared open-mouthed at the forest of dark legs skirted, wrapped and panted in every variety of stripe and color. Woven baskets bounced on hips, filled with everything from cabbages to chickens to Coke cans. Rosaries swung in the folds of black habits. He peered out from behind the big wheels, soaking in a whole new world.

The streets teemed with more people than Raul knew existed. Stepping out into the sun, he felt suddenly sick. How stupid he had been! This was nothing like his village, and he would never find his mother! The other boys were already gone, having jumped at the first light of dawn while he slept. Raul stared at the loud, pulsing crowd. He had never felt so alone.

With nowhere to go, Raul simply walked until he found himself at Mexico City's grand palace park. He slumped down on a bench, tired, hungry and scared.

"Amigo!" a little hand prodded him with curious persistence. "What are you doing here?"

Suddenly, a flock of ragged children appeared and surrounded the newcomer.

"Where's your family? Do you have anywhere to go?"

Raul shrugged. "No."

"Do you have somewhere to sleep?"

"Got anything to eat?"

"No."

"What are you going to do?" A tiny girl with wide brown eyes and a runny nose tugged at his sleeve.

"I'm going to die." He said it with unfeeling resignation.

"No, you're not." The little girl curled her fingers around his and smiled shyly. "You can stay with us."

In a chorus of agreement, the bedraggled gang repeated her invitation.

"We're just like you." A slightly bigger boy took in Raul's scars with a knowing glance. "Look." He shoved up his sleeve, exposing a row of cigarette burns.

"We don't have anybody either," another chimed in.

In a moment, they were all showing Raul their various scars and injuries, each knowing well the comfort of common misfortune.

This group of abandoned and runaway children in Parque Alameda Central became Raul's family for the next ten years. They taught him to shine shoes for pesos, pick pockets and beg from street vendors. He learned that sometimes people could be merciful, like the ones who stopped for a shine even though their shoes were perfectly clean. And like the newspaper vendor who left his stall unlocked, knowing the children came at night seeking shelter from the cold.

The park fountain provided a place to occasionally wash away the humiliating dirt and smell that made people turn away in disgust. After dark, the children would take turns standing guard, then bathing. Above all, they did not want to get caught by the police who often demanded money in exchange for their freedom.

Raul gave up looking for his mother. The quest was just too hopeless in this city of millions. However, bitterness and anger consumed him as he grew. Daily he cursed his mother for leaving him and longed for a normal life and home.

At nineteen, he met a crew of bricklayers and saw his opportunity to escape the misery of the street. They offered to train him and he accepted the job, following them around the city and sleeping at job sites. After two weeks, Raul received his first real wages.

Most of the money was spent. Raul walked through the storefront doors bursting with pride. His clothes smelled new and felt stiff after wearing rags for so many years. He walked, almost running, for the park. What would his friends think? He laughed to himself. This was a happy day. With the few pesos left, he would buy everyone a hot churro or maybe a sweet, sticky tamarindo for the little ones. He began to run as the park came into view.

"Letty! Manuel!" He cupped his mouth and shouted again.

No familiar faces popped from behind the trees. Raul ran to the fountain plaza, darting between strolling mothers and lunching secretaries.

"Carlos! 'Pita!" He imagined the look on their faces when they first saw him and he smiled again. "Where are you?"

An hour later, Raul sagged against the main gate. He had been through two miles of park and had run up and down the main street. Perspiration soaked his new shirt. His friends – where were they? He began to frantically question the street hawkers, the sidewalk artists – anyone who might have seen his "family".

"Can't you tell me anything? What happened?" Raul wanted to shake the gardener. The old man just backed away, dropping his head and mumbling something Raul could not understand.

For the next year, Raul spent every Sunday off looking for his vanished friends throughout the city, but he never saw those children nor heard of them again.

A few months passed. Raul squinted in the Sunday afternoon sun, straining to catch another glimpse of a blue, striped T-shirt as it disappeared into a thicket of shoppers. Manny? Manny had a shirt like that. Another weekend, another day of looking. He could not give up. The boy in the blue shirt reappeared, holding the hand of a stout woman carrying a baby on her back. Raul blinked back his tears. This was ridiculous. But he had nowhere else to go, no one else who mattered.

Suddenly, there it was – the face from his aunt's tattered photo. Raul's heart jumped and he could hardly breathe. His mother! Shoving his way through the crowd, he kept his eyes riveted to her form, afraid she would be swallowed up and lost to him again. He hadn't seen her since he was three and he hadn't seen the photo since he was five. Could he be mistaken?

He touched the woman's shoulder and she jerked around with a scowl.

"Are you Maria Lopez Jimenez?" He stared at every detail of her face. The woman squirmed under the scrutiny.

"Yeah, I am. Who the hell are you?"

"Are you from Capulalpan de Mendez in Oaxaca?" Raul had to be sure.

"That's right. How do you know that?"

"Did you leave a son with your mother about 17 years ago?"

The woman stared back at Raul. He thought he could detect a slight relaxing, a softening in her hostile eyes.

"Yes, I had a son . . ."

"I am your son! Raul!" He waited awkwardly for some response.

"Raul," she mumbled. "Mother Mary, I can't believe . . ."

" . . . I found you? I looked for many years but gave up a long time ago. Isn't this incredible? We've found each other and now we can be together again!" For one moment, a great surging hope engulfed all Raul's years of hatred. He wanted nothing more than to go with this woman, to pretend his life hadn't happened the way it did, and be a family.

"I never expected to . . ." She began to pull away as Raul interrupted.

"Of course, you couldn't have expected to find me. You had no idea where I was." Oh, how he wanted to believe she had looked for him.

"Listen, that was a long time ago. I've got a new life, a husband, children." She turned to go.

"Wait!" Raul couldn't believe what was happening. Was she really going to just leave? "Take me with you," he managed to say. "I won't be any trouble. I have a job. I can help. We can get to know each other again . . . please."

She stopped abruptly and faced Raul. "You're not my son," she lied. "I found you in the garbage." Her face contorted and Raul felt spit on his cheek. "Now leave me alone!"

Despite the anguish of that encounter, Raul determined to try again. The very next day, after collecting his last paycheck, he returned to his aunt's home in Oaxaca and told her about the meeting. She wrote to Raul's mother, urging her to come home but not telling her Raul was there to see her.

A week later, Raul heard she had arrived. He hurried up the jungled hillside, panting by the time he reached his aunt and uncle's house. It sat just off the dirt road that wound through the mountains and, finally, into Oaxaca City itself. As soon as he arrived, he sensed something had gone wrong.

"Is she here?" His aunt stood in the yard, shaking her head. "Did she come?"

"She came." She folded her thick arms across her chest. "You should have listened, Raul. She doesn't want you."

Raul stared down the empty road, thinking of his prepared words, words to convince her, to awaken her mother's heart, all prepared for nothing. "She left?"

His uncle emerged from the dark, low entry of the house. "She's too smart for you," he laughed. "She figured it out and took the first bus back."

His grandmother sat on an overturned bucket, fanning herself in the shade of the banana trees. She raised a bony finger in his direction. "If she loved you, she would have waited. Now forget it."

His aunt agreed. "You're a fool if you think you can change her mind."

"The boy is a fool! Look at him." Raul could see now that his uncle was drunk. "A stupid idiot, crying for his mother. Well, she's gone. Got that? She doesn't want anything to do with you and she's gone."

They could hear the rough rattling of a pick-up truck laboring up the mountain. They heard it reach the nearest point to the house. Raul dashed for the road. On a desperate impulse, he lunged for the tailgate and threw himself in. If he could just talk to her again, she would have to listen!

The truck pulled into Oaxaca City and Raul jumped out, heading for the main bus station. He found a bus with "Mexico City" displayed in the header, scheduled to leave after dark. When the opportunity came, he scrambled into the cargo hold of the bus, squeezing himself into the few inches that remained between piles of luggage below him and the floor of the bus above him.

For nine endless hours, he choked on exhaust fumes, his head throbbing from the loud roar of the motor. Hunger, an unrelieved bladder and the fear of being caught all kept him awake and miserable.

The Mexico City terminal was too busy for anyone to notice the young man crawling out from the luggage hold. Raul straightened and gasped, delighted at his good luck. There, getting off the same bus, stepped his mother. He slipped into the crowd behind her and followed her home.

Nothing turned out as he hoped. Enraged by his arrival at her house, his mother grabbed the extension cord from an iron and began to flail at Raul until his back and arms were covered with cuts from the prongs. Finally, her husband stepped in.

"It's better for you to leave," he muttered. His voice was heavy with apology. "She doesn't love you and I can't do anything for you."

Despondent, Raul joined the army. He made just enough pay to become a heavy drinker and was dishonorably discharged after two years for alcoholism. By then, his desire to be reunited with his mother had been replaced with an obsessive hatred. He spent his days planning her murder. She had a new address that his relatives refused to give him. However, there was one place she would eventually, inevitably return to, he thought. He went back to their home town in Oaxaca ... to wait.

In the small town of Capulalpan de Mendez, Raul found a job with the local police force. His drinking continued as he sank into isolation, living in a rented room and estranged from his relatives.

During this season, Raul remembered his childhood dream of the man robed in white. "So much time has gone by," he prayed, "it has taken me until now to remember You." He knew nothing, except that God existed and he began to cry out to this unknown Being.

The morning sun spilled across his dark brown skin, leaving a shimmer of perspiration in its path. Raul readjusted his hat and settled himself for an early nap.

"Are you Raul Garcia?"

Raul opened one sleepy eye. A man with a briefcase strode toward him across the weed-infested yard.

Instinctively, Raul reached for his gun. "How do you know my name?"

The man kept walking without hesitation. "The Lord sent me to talk to you about the gospel."

"Who is this 'Lord?'" Actually, Raul felt more irritation than curiosity.

"The Lord Jesus." Now he stood in front of Raul's chair, blocking the sun. "He called me out of my house, told me your name and what you would be wearing and described this house. You must go to His feet and repent."

"Look, I'm a police officer. I don't have time to talk to you." Raul eyed the briefcase. Was this man a lunatic? A debt collector? His hand closed around the handle of the revolver in his belt.

The man paused, obviously not enthused about his assignment. "Fine. I've done what God told me to do. If you don't want to listen, that's up to you. The rest is your fault. One day, if you want to find me, I live down the road."

Raul relaxed, anxious to be left alone again, and waved him off. "Fine."

One night a month later, Raul could not sleep. Thoughts of his strange visitor haunted him. Who had told him all those details about him, what he would be wearing, where he lived? Finally, he fell asleep wondering about the "Lord" that had sent him. That night, Raul saw the man in white from his childhood dream again. This time, the man spoke.

"I'm looking for you."

Suddenly Raul remembered the words of the man who lived down the road.

"Lord, I know You are Jesus! Forgive me. I have failed You." Raul cried out, wanting to jump up and stay forever in the mysteriously comforting presence of this man. "From now on, I will follow You."

"No, go and tell your family."

Raul's aunt and uncle didn't know what to make of the dream, but felt sure they should all go to church. They rarely went themselves, but it was after all, Christmas Eve. During the entire three-hour walk to church, Raul's heart raged with conflicting emotions. "Church is for saints, people who never do anything bad, not for people like me." But he had seen Jesus! Raul felt feverish and confused. At the church door, several men greeted them and invited them in. With great reluctance, Raul entered.

Instantly, he felt something in his soul. "This is what I've been looking for my whole life," he thought, but didn't dare say it to his aunt or uncle. Raul left the Christmas Eve service in turmoil. The gospel seemed like a door that would surely slam in his face. He was a drunk with no job and had murder in his heart. His own mother and family had rejected him. Why would God accept him? Nevertheless, he asked the church for a Bible and began to read.

One night in January, Raul went to bed telling God, "If the door was open for me, I would walk in. But it's not for me."

For the third time, God visited Raul supernaturally.

"Get up!" The voice woke Raul and he sat up. Two men stood by his bed, one at the head and one at the foot. Their faces were dark, Oaxacan faces like his, but their clothing shone with dazzling, white light.

"Open your Bible," one instructed, "The good works of righteous people will not save them if they turn to sin, nor will the sins of evil people destroy them if they repent and turn from their sins."

Raul jumped up and grabbed his Bible. As it opened, his eyes fell on the man's exact words in Ezekiel 33:12.

Raul stammered, "This is for me?"

"Yes, for you."

Overwhelmed by a powerful sense of God's grace, Raul bowed his head and wept with joy. When he looked up again, the men were gone.

The pastor at the church Raul attended on Christmas Eve agreed to baptize Raul at Easter, waiting to make sure his conversion was genuine and not just the hallucination of a drunk. Shortly after, a man from town offered to pay Raul's tuition to Bible school in Oaxaca City. The classes demanded more education than Raul had ever received. Through prayer and fasting, Raul learned to depend upon God for understanding, even for the ability to read and write. But after two years, the scholarship funds disappeared and Raul sought God to open a new door.

With his heart on fire for Jesus, Raul went to work picking in the tomato fields of Sinaloa. There he preached the gospel to any fellow workers who would listen. Following the various crops, he eventually ended up harvesting melon seeds in the San Quintin valley of Baja. Living in the Rancho Milagro camp for migrant laborers, he formed a small "church" of sixteen people he had led to Christ. He dreamt, literally, of returning to Bible school. In his dream, he arrived at a school dirty, hungry and broke, but was received and allowed to study. When he awoke, Raul dismissed it as an impossibility.

One day a local pastor visited the camp for the first time and asked if there was anyone who wanted to study the Bible. Later he returned with an application, telling Raul that God had led him to the camp to find him. He came back the next day, drove Raul to the school at FFHM's mission and dropped him off. Raul had nothing but a nylon sack with two pairs of pants. He had no tuition money nor a pastor's referral as required on the application. The man's truck roared away in a cloud of dust and Raul wondered if he had made another foolish mistake. Of course, they would reject him. But as he began to look around, he realized he was seeing the very buildings from his Bible school dream.

Within moments, a man approached. "Are you Raul Garcia?"

Raul nodded.

"God told me you were coming. How about a shower and something to eat?"

Raul graduated from Bible school two years later and continued to preach in the camps, leading many to Christ. He is a gentle, affectionate man with a beaming smile – a transformed man who bears little resemblance to his former self. He speaks of his first years at the mission with deep emotion.

"This is where God showed me the condition of my heart . . . that it was still in pieces and full of hatred, bitterness and unforgiveness."

Charla remembers when Raul could not even talk about his past. "My heart was a locked room," Raul agrees, "I didn't want anyone; I said I didn't need anyone. Little by little, my heart opened as God loved me through the people here. My wounds were healed. With Christ, there is a future and a hope! If I could find my real mother today, I would tell her I have forgiven her."

After Raul married, he and his wife Flor served for many years as houseparents at the mission orphanage. Many of those in his care were interned because of abandonment and/or abuse.

"I understand the pain these children feel," he explains. "But I am an example of how God seeks what has been rejected by others. He is the great healer. He binds up the broken-hearted!"

*"Can a **mother** forget the baby at her breast*
and have no compassion on the child she has borne?
Though she may forget,
I will not forget you!"
(Isaiah 49:15)

Chapter 2

Out of the Darkness

"Some became fools through their rebellious ways
and suffered affliction because of their iniquities.
They loathed all food
and drew near the gates of death.
Then they cried to the LORD in their trouble,
and he saved them from their distress.
He sent forth his word and healed them;
he rescued them from the grave.
Let them give thanks to the LORD for his unfailing love
and his wonderful deeds for men.
Let them sacrifice thank-offerings
and tell of his works with songs of joy."
(Psalm 107:17–22)

The little girl wiped her eyes with the back of her grimy, torn sleeve. Smoke from the dump fires made her eyes sting but she didn't want to leave yet. She poked with her stick through moldy orange rinds and the contents of an office wastebasket. Paper, paper, half a snapped pencil, a pen ... did it still work? There must be something here worth pocketing to sell on the streets tomorrow.

"Alma, look!" Her little brother's hand emerged from a pile of kitchen scraps clutching a half-eaten taco. Flies buzzed around his sticky fingers and finally settled on his prize find.

"No!" Alma slapped his hand and sent the garbage flying. "It's already got worms. Keep looking."

She couldn't look into his face, even when he began to cry. She was tired of looking at hunger, tired of sickness, just tired of everything. Darkness began to creep across the sky and the mounds of decay around her threw deepening shadows. They needed to go while they could still tell an old shoe from a rat.

"Go home," she ordered. The little boy stared at her, knowing she wouldn't be coming along. Actually, he wasn't her brother at all, but just one of the many children Alma's mother cared for while their real mothers worked the streets. Sullenly, he turned to go and Alma began to run the other way.

Run! If she could just run far enough, could she run away from hell? Where was there to go? It was all around her, even at home. Home was that place she didn't dare sleep because of the intruders, those men her mother brought home that intruded upon her bed, her body. Alma was ten and hadn't slept through the night since two months before her sixth birthday – the first night of countless rapes. Where was there to run? Her older sisters were already on the streets, living her inevitable future. Alma ran until she stumbled and fell against the rusting, peeling paint of an abandoned car. She pulled at the sagging door and fell onto the torn, stained upholstery. She would sleep here tonight.

Morning brought visitors to the Ensenada city dump. Alma watched the van winding and lurching through the hilly terrain of broken bottles and plastic trash. A cross and dove had been painted on the sides, the cross splitting in two when the sliding door opened. Like dozens of other hopeful, hungry children, Alma scurried to get in line. A newer car, at least one that ran and had the name of a church on it, always meant food. Someone reached out with a turkey sandwich and Alma grabbed it. If there was candy, she'd save it for one of the younger ones at home.

Pretty soon, the people from inside the car were talking about God and telling stories. She listened carefully. If she could answer the questions at the end, there would be a prize. "How did God save the Israelites from Pharoah's army?" She was good at this. She had already won a notebook and pen for school. If it weren't for these silly stories and contests, she wouldn't have any of the supplies she needed. If they wanted her to answer questions, fine, as long as they had prizes.

But sometimes they asked the kids to raise their hands if they believed in Jesus. Who were they trying to kid? Could they really be so stupid? So blind? All you had to do was look around. "If there is a God," Alma wanted to ask, "how can you explain my life?" But she never asked, afraid the sandwiches might stop. Sometimes she even let them pray for her, standing quietly as some well-intentioned woman laid hands on her head, praying to a God that Alma was sure did not exist.

She was twelve the day she fell in love with drugs.

She knew several of her "brothers" were living in this house but no one was home. What were these? A pile of capsules lay scattered on the table. Well, what did it matter? At worst, she would die and death was a welcome consequence. She got a glass of water. By the time anyone came home, the deepest sleep of Alma's life had engulfed her in soft, dark billows of dreamless silence. This must be heaven! No nightmares, no fear, no hunger – just wonderful sleep. For 24 hours, her panicking brothers tried to wake her, afraid she would die or remain in a coma. When she finally woke, Alma knew one thing. She knew how to escape from hell!

That year brought the startling revelation that she was an adopted child. For Alma, that explained everything – why her mother didn't love her, why she constantly called her a "curse," blaming her for her adoptive father's death shortly after her arrival, why she ignored the molestation, saying a bad person deserved whatever evil befell her. Alma had no more reason to go home, ever.

The gang loved Alma. She would and could do just about anything. She burned with a hatred that consumed any possible remorse. She acted with a recklessness only seen in those who want to die. Carrying drugs and money with cool ease, she was frequently assigned to dangerous border crossings. She learned quickly from her customers and soon spoke fluent English. Even though she was jailed and beaten many times, no serious charges ever stuck and the police hated her for that. But one day everything changed . . .

Martin, her main supplier, was sweating, rubbing his palms on expensive trousers. He wouldn't open the door far enough for Alma to get in and this irritated her.

"I have to come in!" she snapped. Her own nerves were screaming for more heroine. What was he trying to pull? She pushed against the door.

"I can't help you anymore. I'm sorry."

"What the hell are you talking about?"

"Alma, you have to go, you have to hide. Now!"

Alma stared at his eyes. They were blinking too fast and he was licking his lips. Martin didn't lick his lips. Something was wrong. Martin had always been there for her, always able to get the drugs she needed. Quickly she reached one hand behind her for the switchblade in her waistband. If there were police behind that door . . .

"What are you doing?" she hissed. She grabbed his wrist with her other hand and squeezed hard. "Tell me!"

Martin winced but avoided her stare. "I made a deal. I had to. Two names for my life. They've already arrested Carlos. I'm giving them your name in the morning. You have 24 hours to get lost." He wrenched his arm free. "I'm sorry!" The door slammed.

Through a friend, Alma found refuge at a well-hidden commune tucked in a canyon outside of Ensenada. She glared at the faces surrounding the campfire. What did these hippies know about life? They were rich kids with nothing better to do than smoke their parents' money. They talked of loving each other. She would just have to bear it, all their stoned philosophizing, at least until the police lost interest in her and she could return to the city.

But that guy over there, the one who came to visit friends, Marco Angulo, what did he want? He was so nice to her and treated her with such respect. Alma withdrew into her quiet suspicions.

Suddenly Marco was next to her, inviting her to walk with him. She mumbled and stared harder at the fire. He ignored her rudeness and asked again, even more gently.

Hours later, they were still walking and Marco was still listening. Alma thought his interest would dissipate as soon as he knew her past, but he only wanted to know more. As her feelings poured out for the first time in memory, Marco cried with her.

Communal life passed, weeks into months, a dreamy parade of mystical debates, prayer, even Bible reading – all blurred by the perpetual marijuana haze that hung over their minds. Marco returned to his parents' home in Ensenada. Alma had his address and promised to come, some day. But not today.

Today, Alma was going to find her mother. Nervously, she checked her backpack for her jacket, some food and enough pot to keep her calm. It would be an eight-hour walk over the mountains – the hippies did not believe in using cars or anything man-made.

Her plan to visit her mother and return to the commune might have worked if she hadn't stopped at her brothers' house. There they were, sitting at the table, slowly, gently grinding down stones of concentrated heroine. The fine powder released a strong, distinct aroma that instantly grabbed at Alma, overwhelming her with a nostalgic pull that she could not break free of.

Alma's eyes opened, slowly focusing on what turned out to be an IV tube. She followed the plastic snake until she saw where it disappeared into her wrist. She groaned in disgust, overdose. She tried to turn her head. Instantly, a wave of nausea ended any thought of moving. A door handle turned and footsteps came closer. Alma waited for a white coat to enter her field of vision. What would it be this time? A lecture? Threats?

Suddenly, her heart pounded with adrenaline. There were no doctors in here. These were the police! Several dark uniforms stopped in front of her, one with a holstered gun she could see just above the rim of her pillow. They spoke in quick, rough tones. There was a short debate about whether or not to handcuff her to the bed. No, she was too sick to worry about it. In a moment they left, posting a guard at the door behind them.

Alma kept her eyes shut to lessen the pain, but her mind scrambled for clarity. She had to get out of here! Martin! She hadn't thought of him in so long. Martin had named her as a key figure in their drug ring. This time it would be no 15 or 30-day sentence. They would put her away for years.

As the morning crept by, Alma concentrated on the door. Did the guard ever leave? No, when he went on a break, another took his place. Only nurses came and went.

"Are you feeling any better?" A starched white dress hovered over the bed.

Alma looked for the face above the uniform. A familiar face! Her brother's old girlfriend, Juanita, smiled down at Alma.

"I thought it was you." Juanita took Alma's hand. "They don't know I know you. Can I get you anything?"

"Yeah. Get me out of here."

"I wish I could. You're in it deep now."

"You have to help me! Juanita, this is it. They'll put me away for good." She clutched at Juanita's arm. "Please!"

Juanita looked miserably torn. What could she do? She could lose her job, but then, if the old gang heard she had refused to help one of their own, that could be even worse.

"What do you expect me to do? Make you disappear?"

"Start with this." Alma began to pull the IV out of her arm. "I've got an idea."

A few minutes later, Juanita was chatting amiably with the guard. Soon Alma could hear flirtatious laughing, Juanita inviting him to a cup of coffee, then the coy suggestion of something more than coffee. The guard peered anxiously into the room. Alma breathed soundly, letting one arm drop limply over the side of the bed. Satisfied, the guard leered at Juanita and the two of them headed down the hall.

Fighting off her dizziness and nausea, Alma fled the hospital and made her way to Marco's address. It was five a.m. and a sleepy, older woman answered the door but Alma shoved past her, screaming for Marco to wake up.

That night, they were alone at the commune. Everyone had gone home to family for Christmas Eve. Marco brought food from home, watching over her with a tenderness she had never known. He promised to take care of her forever. It was a love Alma didn't know how to receive. "This is a good man," she thought. "Too good to have his life ruined by someone like me."

Marco didn't know what to do with his new wife; Alma was high again. He couldn't leave their baby alone with her and he couldn't stay with her every moment either. His father refused to let them move in with them. His parents were already outraged that he had married Alma, dashing their dreams of medical school and a respectable future.

In spite of Marco's best efforts, Alma sank into deep depression. She didn't know how to deal with the bitterness and hatred that haunted her, except to mask her feelings with more drugs. Her addiction drove Alma back to the streets where she could earn the money her husband wouldn't give her. Finally, Marco conceded defeat. Taking their daughter to his parents' home to stay, he left for medical school in Mexicali. He came home once a month to visit. When he came, Alma acted as normal as possible, not wanting him to know how really desperate her lifestyle was. If he knew, he might drop out of school and try to save her again. She knew it was hopeless. It was better this way. Eventually, after four years, Alma got what she wanted – Marco separated and divorce papers were started.

The gun was easy to get. Now it sat on the kitchen table, waiting for her. She just needed to write a letter to her daughter, to tell her she was removing the "curse" from her life.

Suddenly, a car pulled up and doors slammed. Alma swept the gun under a sofa cushion. Familiar voices at the door made her freeze, listening in astonishment. What were they doing here? Benito and Rosa Maria had been the leaders of the hippie commune, her friends during what now seemed like another lifetime. She answered the door before they had a chance to knock.

"Alma, thank God you're okay!" Rosa Maria threw her arms around Alma.

"I can't believe we found you!" Benito echoed his wife's relief. "We've been looking for you."

This unexpected visit caught Alma off guard and she struggled to bring her mind back from the brink of suicide. "What are you doing here?" she stammered and pulled away from Rosa Maria's embrace.

"Can we sit down?" Benito asked. "We have a lot to talk about."

Alma thought the whole conversation strange. Rosa Maria talked about a dream. In the dream, she had seen Alma about to shoot herself. After the third time she had this same dream, she realized God was speaking to her, telling her to find Alma.

God was speaking to Rosa Maria? Alma snorted. Yet, she was strangely touched by their concern and startled by the accuracy of Rosa Maria's dream. Why did they look so different? She hardly recognized them. Their faces radiated a peace Alma had never seen before.

"Come on, guys," Alma badgered, "what great drug have you discovered now?"

"No drugs, Alma," Benito answered seriously but with a smile, "just Jesus."

"We've given our lives to Jesus, Alma. He's the reason we're here. He loves you and He can save you, if you'll let Him."

She'd heard enough! Alma didn't want saving, not now, not ever. Why hope in someone that didn't exist for something that wasn't possible? This was how she lived; this was how she'd die.

Benito and Rosa Maria continued to share with Alma, telling her about their new life in Christ. Alma let her mind drift back into its own shadows and the couple's words spilled to the floor like crumbs to sweep up later ... maybe. Finally they left, wondering if Alma had listened to anything they said.

Alma hid the gun away and two weeks passed. Something stopped her from taking it out again, but she didn't know what. Was it something her friends had said? Not likely. The place in her heart that might have reached out to God had long since turned to stone. Still, there was a new restlessness, like she was groping hungrily for some new possibility, something that waited out there in the dark.

Well, tonight she knew one thing. She needed to make some money before her fix wore off. Then she'd find Marco and get him to sign the final divorce papers that had just arrived.

Alma headed for the lights of downtown, first turning down a dark sidestreet, then cutting across the auto repair lot. She walked a little faster to warm up her bare legs. Car horns blared and Latin disco music blasted from various storefronts.

Suddenly, Alma became aware of one sound distinguished from the others. Singing. Maybe she noticed it because it was so oddly out of place. As she listened, she heard words and phrases that she recognized ... from where? Benito and Rosa Maria were talking about this stuff! The words spoke of a great love, the love of God, of One who offered forgiveness. Strangely drawn by the music, Alma followed it to its source and found herself at a little Pentecostal church where 20–30 people were pouring their hearts out in worship. Worship? Alma's heart pounded. She couldn't understand what was happening inside her. Part of her longed to be here and another part of her boiled up in rage. If God existed, He was a cruel God and certainly not deserving of worship! "How can these people sing," she wondered, "when so much pain and misery surrounds them?" Angry and frustrated, Alma left.

She went back though, each time just listening to the music. On her third visit, a preacher came to the pulpit and Alma turned to flee.

"I think you should stay."

"No way!" The words flew from Alma's mouth before she realized it was a little grandmother speaking to her. "Sorry Granny, but this isn't for me."

"Oh, yes it is." Alma was shocked at the old woman's firmness. "You're a drug addict, aren't you?" the woman boldly persisted. "And a prostitute. You need to listen, so just sit down!"

Alma fidgeted, but for some reason, she couldn't move. The old woman practically pushed her into a seat at the back of the room.

As the preacher continued to speak with increasing fervor, Alma sat stunned. The preacher was talking about her! Marco must have spoken to him. How dare he! And here the preacher was telling a room full of strangers about her. Angry, she tried again to leave.

But again, the old woman came to her side and stopped her. "So you think you're pretty tough, don't you?" she asked. "Not afraid of anything?"

"Tough enough!" Alma snapped, heading for the door.

"Really? Let's see how brave you are. Are you brave enough to meet your Creator? Just you and Him?"

Alma looked around for an escape. The preacher was asking people to come to the altar and pray.

"Come on," the woman urged, nodding towards the altar.

"I'm **not** going down there!" Alma hissed.

"Yes, you are!"

Somehow, Alma knew she was not arguing with just an old woman who barely knew her. Some other mysterious authority compelled her to the altar.

"Kneel down."

"I'm **not** going to kneel down!"

"Yes, you are!"

It was useless to fight any longer. Alma fell to her knees and, suddenly, no one else was in the room. God alone met with her. Alma wept and wept as walls of resistance came crashing down for the first time since she was five years old. From the deepest places of her wounded spirit, came a desperate cry to a God that might exist, that might care enough about her to help her. As waves of emotion convulsed through her body, she could put just one simple prayer into words: "God, if You're really there, help me. Help me sleep tonight without taking any drugs." It was both a plea and a challenge.

That night, Alma sat on her bedside staring at 30 milligrams of valium and a glass of water. Beside the valium, lay the half spoon of cocaine she would need to get up in the morning. Day and night, this had been her bondage for the last eleven years. Without it, she could neither sleep nor wake. Would tonight be different? Again, Alma challenged God to set her free.

Sunlight streamed through faded curtains and warmed her face. Alma woke with a start. What time was it? Six a.m.! The valium and water still sat on the lamp table, untouched. She couldn't remember anything after . . . after asking God to put her to sleep. Alma jumped up, more frightened than she had ever been in her life. God was real! This was scary! Her heart pounded as all the implications ran through her mind. She needed to repent!

But this was wonderful, too. Scary and wonderful at the same time. It meant God was with her, He was on her side after all. If God was going to help her, she could do anything, even beat the drugs! As if she had just woken from an eleven-year coma, Alma's heart surged with all the new possibilities of life. She had a daughter. She could live!

A short time later, Marco returned from Mexicali, radiating a joy Alma had never seen. Marco told his own incredible story of an encounter with God while studying for a test in his grand-mother's backyard (see Chapter 10). He pulled Alma into his big embrace. "Honey, we need to start over. God is with us!"

A new beginning

That year, Marco and Alma Angulo renewed their marriage vows and brought their daughter home to stay. They began to build a new life centered on their relationship with Jesus.

Having finished medical school with a specialty in family practice, Marco was sent to administer a medical clinic in Jalisco. They knew of no other Christians in their small, seaside village of 3,000 so the Angulos began to share their faith and started a small church with friends they led to Christ.

In 1994, the Angulos moved back to the San Quintin Valley to be near Marco's dying father. One day Alma decided to look up an old friend from Ensenada, Maria Rodriquez. She had heard Maria was working as a dentist at an orphanage somewhere in the valley.

On Alma's second visit, Marco insisted on coming along and met Dr. Luc Chaussé. The two doctors each discovered an instant soulmate in the other and Dr. Marco longed to join Dr. Luc in his work, even though it would mean giving up his government position. Dr. Luc was about to return to Canada and he saw Dr. Marco's arrival as an answer to his prayer for a replacement.

But Alma didn't want to come! Helping out was one thing, but live by faith working in a free clinic? They would never have the things she enjoyed as a doctor's wife. After a lifetime of poverty, how could God ask her to let it all go now?

Terrified that Marco would throw away his career for the life of a missionary, Alma began to pack. They would move back to Mexicali she thought, and forget about all this. She wanted to devote her life to her own family, creating the type of home she had never had as a child.

But Marco knew God's call and he began to pray, asking God to change Alma's heart. One day, Alma was introduced to Charla. As others in the room chatted, Alma stared at this Anglo woman, trying to place her strangely familiar face. Could she be . . . ?

"Sister Charla," Alma suddenly interrupted, "did you use to go by the Anza theater in Ensenada about 25 years ago?"

"Yes," Charla answered, surprised, "our attorney's office was next door to the theater and I went there often. We were working on getting our Foundation's license."

"It was you!" Old memories of bitter, sad days suddenly resurfaced and tears began to flow. Alma could barely speak. "I was the little beggar girl on the corner. Sometimes I sold tortillas." Alma gazed out the office window at children playing in the safety of the yard, shoes on their feet, a meal waiting in the dining hall. She turned back to Charla with brimming eyes that asked more than her words. "Why didn't you bring me here?"

That day, Alma knew God was calling her to the mission. Every little child rescued from the dump, every child brought to the orphanage because of abandonment or abuse was another little Alma. Jesus was asking her to make a difference in that child's life.

Marco and Alma worked together in the mission's medical clinic for several years and often ministered in the camps with a deep compassion for the destitute.

Could Alma ever go back to being "just a doctor's wife"? Alma shakes her head. "Going to the camps is painful. I don't just see a need or an injustice. I see myself and I feel what they feel. It would be easier to run away from it. But my personal feeling is this – you can't be a Christian and live like there's nothing going on out there."

As hostess for visiting groups, Alma always prayed that God would implant His heart in those who came. She explains, "Sometimes teams come for a short time and wonder if they really make a difference. Well, when some kid gets one sandwich in a month, believe me, even that makes a difference. I know. I was that kid."

"We have escaped like a bird
out of the fowler's snare;
the snare has been broken,
and we have escaped.
Our help is in the name of the LORD,
the Maker of heaven and earth."
(Psalm 124:7–8)

Chapter 3

Free at Last

"Some sat in darkness and the deepest gloom,
  prisoners suffering in iron chains,
for they had rebelled against the words of God
  and despised the counsel of the Most High.
So he subjected them to bitter labor;
  they stumbled, and there was no-one to help.
Then they cried to the LORD in their trouble,
  and he saved them from their distress.
He brought them out of darkness and the deepest gloom
  and broke away their chains.
Let them give thanks to the LORD for his unfailing love
  and his wonderful deeds for men,
for he breaks down gates of bronze
  and cuts through bars of iron."
                    (Psalm 107:10–16)

"Papa, I just need ten cents," Glen muttered, "just ten cents."

"You don't need nothin'!" His father slammed the refrigerator door, then held onto it for an extra second to regain his balance.

"Yes, I do. I need to buy a new pencil."

"You hear me? I said you don't need nothin'!"

The twelve-year-old boy edged for the screen door, not willing to give up, but not stupid either. Best to plan for a quick escape if necessary.

"I need it for school. Come on, it's just a dime."

The ash tray just missed his head and smashed into the wall

behind him, leaving a patch of chipped paint smeared with gray. Glen kicked at a shard of green glass.

"Just great. Mom would've really been impressed."

"Shut up about your mother!"

"Why? She was my mother. She would've given me the stupid dime!" Suddenly Glen too, wished he hadn't brought up his mother. It was still too soon, too painful.

"You still yappin' about that dime? I swear, I'm gonna ... "

The only way to keep from crying was to scream.

"You're gonna what? What? Get another beer, that's all you're gonna do! That's all you ever do!"

His father lunged forward and Glen opened the screen door, darting behind it. His father's hand reached for the frame just as Glen slammed it shut. Yelping with pain, the man punched his other fist straight through the nylon mesh and grabbed his terrified son by a handful of hair. Glen kicked and flailed, his whole body electrified by frustration and rage.

His father's voice trembled as he hissed in Glen's face. "Get outta here, you hear me? Get outta my sight and don't you ever come back!"

He released his grip and Glen ran from the house.

The family had moved from Tijuana to San Diego when Glen was seven. He was eleven before anyone tried to put him back in school. Hopelessly behind his sixth-grade classmates, Glen gave up and refused to go. Now he lived on the streets. Quickly, life turned into a cycle of incarcerations and paroles as Glen became a regular in the San Diego Juvenile Detention system – a fourteen-year-old, gang-banging heroine addict.

Tonight, the icy wind snaked through the folds of Glen's worn jacket. The sprinklers in the park had left the grass too wet to lie on. Not that he slept much at night anyway. Just too cold. Usually he kept moving, looked for parties, then slept when the sun came up. He slipped into the public toilet, yanked all the paper squares out of the dispenser and lit the pile on the floor. The fire burned down quickly so Glen emptied the paper towel canister as well. When they disappeared in a pile of ash, he ducked into the women's side and took everything he could burn from there. It all lasted just long enough to warm away the shivers. Then the merciless cold crept back, stiffening his fingers and driving him back into the streets to hunt for the "hombres" and enough action to keep his adrenaline running high.

Dawn rose over Chula Vista, a pink halo that crowned the head of the coming sun. Glen and his compadres shuffled down the alley behind Burger King, looking for old buns left by the dumpster. They passed around the beer stolen from 7-Eleven and counted their cash taken from the register.

Glen tossed his empty bottle into the bushes. "Later, man, gotta go see the family."

They were near his older brother's house. Patty, his sister-in-law, felt sorry for Glen and Glen knew how to capitalize on that for a hot meal. He walked in without knocking. "Que pasa?"

"Glen, you look terrible." Luis, his brother, was on his way out, leaving for work.

"No worse than usual." Glen laughed and drifted around the kitchen like a dustball caught in a draft.

"How about some breakfast?" Patty asked, struggling to sound cheerful.

"Why else do you think he's here?" Luis stopped at the door. "Glen, there's a position open at the warehouse. I can put in a word for you. How about it?"

"What's for breakfast?" Glen didn't seem to hear.

"Seriously, Glen. You could stay here again, try again, stay as long as you need to, 'til you get it together."

Patty stared at her husband in disbelief. They had taken Glen in so many times, but it always turned out the same way. He would clean up for a few weeks, maybe a couple of months, then go right back to the heroine. He'd cry, they'd cry, and he'd be gone again. Always, he ended up back in prison. They'd see him again on his next parole.

"Glen!" Luis tried to get his attention. "Listen to me man, you keep living like this, you're gonna die."

"Yeah?" Glen looked up slowly. "So what? This is how I am ... this is how I'll die. Having fun, feeling good ... " He laughed but it rattled empty and humorless.

For Glen, heroine was the real prison. Chino, Donovan and Jamestown State Penitentiaries – they were just places to live out the hours, the days and years of a life he had already given up on.

That year, Glen's girlfriend gave birth to a baby girl. Something began to change in Glen as her new, little life rekindled his longing to live. Suddenly, the winos in the park were not just familiar friends. They were haunting omens of his future. The dead bodies of fellow gang members were not just fallen buddies; they were prophetic signs of his own inevitable end. He wanted out! He wanted his life back! Desperately, Glen began to struggle with his addiction. Over and over, he promised his girlfriend he would change, he would stop the drugs and live a normal life. After his repeated failures, she left him in disgust, taking their daughter to live with her parents.

Paroled again. Sitting in the parked car, Glen glanced quickly in every direction. Why was Paco taking so long? Suddenly, Paco appeared from behind, tossed the shotgun onto the back floor and slid through the driver's side window into his seat with a whoop.

"Score, man!" He threw a paper bag full of bills into Glen's lap. Paco hit the accelerator, tires squealed, and they roared down the narrow street.

They headed straight into a bar of spinning red and blue lights. Glen swore. High beams shone through the windshield, blinding them as Paco slammed on the brakes.

Glen's mind raced. Why were they being stopped? He remembered the shotgun. Parole violation. Why the police cars? Nowhere to run! Nowhere to hide the gun! Two men matching their description were wanted for a murder that weekend in San Diego. He heard the police order, amplified and booming from the row of black and whites. He eased out of the car with all the attitude he could muster and put his hands over his head.

For some inexplicable reason, Glen was released but Paco was held in the County Jail. A month later, Glen came back, arrested this time for possession of stolen goods. His earlier case involving Paco was still before the court. He needed to talk to Paco! What was going on? They met at the only place they could see each other – chapel.

Later, Glen would remember this as the time when the Holy Spirit began to work on his heart. He had no intention of listening to the messages, but still God's Word touched him and a seed was planted. After his transfer to Chino, he continued to attend church there. It didn't last long, though. He quickly realized that many inmates used church as a cover, hiding behind a pretense of conversion and religion. He wanted nothing to do with the games being played and decided not to attend until back on the street. With that decision made, he soon forgot about God altogether.

After a transfer to Jamestown and two more years, Glen was paroled again. He headed for his brother's house, this time really wanting to make it. A week went by.

Glen paced the small house, glancing at the clock for the tenth time in 30 minutes. Finally, he grabbed the phone. There had to be a party somewhere on a Friday night!

Luis looked up from the couch and spoke over the din of the television comedy. "Don't go, Glen ... don't go."

Glen laughed into the receiver. "Sounds good, man. I'll take the trolley." He hung up. "Don't worry. I'm just gonna have a couple of beers, find a girl. I'll be back tonight. If not tonight, in the morning."

Luis turned back to the show, shaking his head in resignation.

The party simmered and churned with young people looking for a reason to be alive. Some needed to prove they were. Some just wanted to escape. Everyone thought a little heroine and beer would help. A fight broke out and Glen pulled his knife. Moments later, he fled the party as an ambulance wailed up to the house for his bloodied friend. He ran until he found his old, homeless amigos on the street. They shared PCP with him until he saw "UFO's" landing just before dawn. Spinning police lights surrounded him. The cops had acted on a call from the victim's mother. Glen went back to prison for three more years.

Glen wore prison life like he wore the tattoos that covered every inch of his upper body – with sullen defiance. Since he could not break free from the heroine and make it on the outside, he decided to make a life for himself on the inside – to become a "lifer." He proved himself a natural leader and soon controlled his yard, deciding where the ever-present stream of drugs would flow. With parole coming up, he planned to make one last visit to his daughter and family. It wouldn't take long he knew, to get sent back to prison for good.

"She's so beautiful!" Glen stared at the little, dark-eyed girl eating at the table. "Hey sweetheart, come say 'hi' to your dad." He held up his hand for a high-five.

The child turned a questioning face to her grandmother. Did she know this man at the door? Grandma nodded her consent, but the girl darted behind the old woman's chair. She peeked out at Glen.

"It's okay. Say 'hi' to your father." She gave Glen a pointed glare. "He has to leave in a minute."

Glen's daughter, Lourdis, hesitated a moment before curiosity took over. She took a few steps out and murmured a soft hello. Glen closed the gap and swung her in his arms until she laughed with glee. When he put her down, tears shone on his cheeks.

"Lupita, I'm going to change. I mean it. I want my daughter." Suddenly his plan for life in prison seemed unbearably empty.

"Bah! I don't want to hear it!" She waved her arms as if warding off a persistent mosquito. "And I don't want her to hear it. No more words."

"I'll change, I promise." The desire to keep his promise squeezed at his heart until it hurt. "I promise."

"How many years have you been saying that?" She shooed him towards the door. "Just do it . . . or don't come back."

Glen felt the punch of her words in his gut. The walls of his prison loomed high and dark around him. He felt like a man scrambling from the bottom of a slippery well. Whatever his desire, his intentions, the walls remained, rising so far that daylight closed to a pinprick hopelessly beyond reach. Within two weeks, Glen had slipped back to the bottom of that well.

But this time, nothing felt the same. The parties didn't cheer him up, the robberies made him feel sick and small inside, the drugs gave him no relief from the guilt that ate at him. The life he once lived without conscience or care now weighed on him like iron chains. Glen fought a powerful urge to simply run into the street screaming, "Someone help me! Help me!" Only the fear of being put into a mental institution stopped him.

He lived in an abandoned car until a friend offered him a couch on the porch. One night, in a frightening dream, he felt his soul leave his body. He woke up terrified and immediately started drinking to calm his fear. The dream repeated itself. Each time, he woke with the fear that his soul would not be able to come back. In a panic, he began to cry out, "God, help me, I'm not going to make it." Suddenly, one morning, he heard himself praying, "God, don't let me die in my sin. Don't let me go to hell." Where did those words come from? Surprised by his own prayer, Glen began to think about the time he attended chapel in prison. He had forgotten about God but now this prayer came from the depths of his heart.

Glen stared dully at passing traffic, finishing off his usual breakfast of two quarts of beer. He hardly noticed the man walking towards him until he spoke. "Is he crazy or just stupid?" Glen thought. The stranger was talking to him about Jesus Christ. In spite of his prayer to God, Glen still thought of Christians as kooks with no real solution for his problems. He didn't even pretend to listen, but sneered and turned away.

"Hey, man, don't you want to change?" The stranger's abrupt question struck hard, penetrating Glen's macho facade. His heart beat faster. A voice screamed inside his head, "Of course, I would **love** to change! But I can't. It's too hard."

Glen turned to the young man, his pride back in place. "No, why should I change?"

Perhaps the man saw the truth in Glen's eyes. He persisted. "If you want, I can help you."

"How can you help me?" Glen scoffed.

"I know a pastor. He has a rehab center. I can take you there."

Glen shrugged. "What do they do there?"

"They read the Bible."

Suddenly Glen burst into hoots of laughter. "Can't you see how I am? How can I go to a place where they read the Bible?"

The man smiled. "Let me explain. There's lots of people there just like you. A lot of people have given their lives to God and Jesus has changed their life."

The words washed over Glen's mind like cool water over a burn – a moment of hope relieving years of despair. Then the sting of countless failures came back. He shoved his hands into his pockets and turned away. "I'll think about it," he lied.

The next day Glen hit the streets again, his body sick with need until he could shoot up with a buddy behind the Circle K convenience store. A couple strolled down the sidewalk and Glen's friend began to flirt crudely with the young senorita in high heels and tight blouse. Within seconds, the scene turned violent as fists flew and knives flashed. Glen's world went black.

A lady's shoe smashed into his temple, bringing him back to consciousness. As his eyes focused, he saw blood covering the body of the man beneath him. The knife in his hand was still embedded in the man's shoulder. Shouts and screams from the small crowd around them filled his ears with a hot roar. Sirens wailed closer. Glen pulled his knife and tore around the corner, down the alley, racing to the pounding of his heart. From a safe distance he watched as an ambulance came for the wounded man. "At least I'm not wanted for murder," he gasped.

The next day, Glen woke up sick again. But this time, his whole being wretched with hunger, not just for drugs, but for relief. For the first time in his life, Glen felt horribly guilty. The weight of it bore down as if the world were shrinking around him and he would suffocate beneath it. Something inside him recognized the weight as the heavy hand of God and he could not bear it. He could hardly breathe. He had to find that Christian from the corner two days ago! Who was he? Where was he? Glen had no idea where to begin looking, so he did the only thing he could think to do – he headed back to the same street where they had met.

"That's the car!" Glen couldn't believe it. He locked eyes with the driver who instantly recognized Glen and slowed down. From all the thousands of cars in downtown traffic, Glen's witnessing "angel" had reappeared the moment Glen reached the corner. Without waiting for the car to stop, Glen yanked open the door and jumped in.

The car turned down a familiar alley and Glen squirmed. The El Shaddai Rehabilitation Center turned out to be just three doors down from his heroine supplier. How could he make it with temptation so close by?

Two days later, the chaplain at El Shaddai gave an altar call. Glen rushed forward, the first to respond.

As Glen tells it, "My life changed completely that day." God helped him through withdrawals with a strength and ease he had never experienced during countless withdrawals in prison. He met scores of other ex-addicts who provided encouragement and inspiration. Most of all, he felt his heart would burst with gratitude. He was free at last!

He developed an insatiable hunger to know God's Word and began to devour its pages. Six weeks later, he preached his first message. When another resident told him afterwards, "God is going to use you," Glen began to wonder about God's plan for his life. Three months later, he felt God telling him to go to Bible school, even promising to help him since he could barely read or write. He wondered if this desire really came from God.

"You're still very young in the Lord, Glen," his director advised him, "Wait a year at least. If you still want to go, then it's the real thing." Over the next year, God's anointing on Glen became obvious to everyone but he struggled with believing in the possibility of Bible school. It seemed hopeless since he lacked both basic education and money.

Glen had been at El Shaddai for a year-and-a-half, and now served as director. Each week, he and twenty men from the rehab center attended a Bible study at Pastor Harald Bredeson's home in San Diego. After the study, the men were paid to work at various jobs on the grounds.

Two acres of pool and gardens sprawled before Glen in the hot, afternoon sun. He pushed the wide broom across terra cotta Mexican pavers, sweeping clipped grass into a neat pile.

"This man will tell you that you are going to be a good pastor."

Glen spun around, looking for the speaker. No one stood behind him. He peered into the bushes, taking a couple of steps in each direction. Feeling a little foolish, he whispered, "Is that You God?" Nah! Were the guys playing a joke? Oh, great. Hearing voices. He acted like nothing had happened and resolved to tell no one. Six months passed.

One day, at the end of a Bible study, Glen headed for the door. "Glen!" Harald greeted Glen with his usual boom of enthusiasm.

"Buenos dias, Pastor." Glen extended his hand to shake. Harald ignored it and hugged Glen instead. Glen still wasn't used to that. One time, Harald had kissed him on the cheek and nearly got punched for it. Glen laughed.

"Glen, sit down please. I want to talk to you. You reflect Jesus in your face. Christians make a big mistake wanting to see Jesus in pictures and paintings. We need to see Jesus in others' faces because He is inside of us." A few moments into the conversation, Pastor Bredesen then asked, "What do you want to do, Glen?"

"I want to preach the gospel."

"I knew it!" Pastor Bredesen beamed with delight. "I have wanted to tell you something for a long time, but I had to wait until I heard those words from your lips. The Lord told me to tell you that you are going to be a good pastor."

Glen nearly choked in surprise. Pastor Bredeson was repeating in English the exact phrase he had mysteriously heard in Spanish months earlier. Glen told the pastor about his earlier experience.

"What do you make of it, Pastor?"

"I think God is calling you and has simply used me to confirm that call."

Two months later, Pastor Bredesen asked Glen again, "What do you want to do?"

"I want to go to Bible school."

"Good, because God has already spoken to me. The Lord told me to send you to a Bible school I know of in a little burg down in the Baja called Colonia Vicente Guerrero."

Mexico! Glen tried not to let the disappointment show on his face. He was a San Diego boy who had never been south of Rosarito Beach. He spoke "Spanglish" – the rough, hybrid language of the street. He felt an instinctive shame and distaste for the poverty and filth that lay just a few miles to the south.

"Really?" Glen tried to act interested. "Well, let me pray about it." Glen returned to the center with no intention of praying. He did not want to go to Mexico!

A week later, as Glen prayed in his office, the Holy Spirit spoke to him the simple phrase, "My will, not yours." Glen began to weep and got on his knees, yielding his life once again. "Lord, I'll go wherever You want me to go, as long as You go with me."

In October of 1992, Max Christian, the administrator of the mission, picked Glen up at El Shaddai and took him to Vicente Guerrero. A week later, Glen was riding his bicycle when a truck went by and threw dirt up into his face. Spitting grit out of his mouth, Glen complained, "God, why am I here in Mexico?"

He wasn't expecting an answer but got one anyway. "I have something for you in Mexico, my son."

Glen started riding again, praising the Lord but wondering what He meant.

Three months after that, a flood came and destroyed the Bible school. Everyone felt the gloom of that day as the relentless rain seemed to wash away every shred of hope. Each minute another chunk of the bank gave way, plunging more walls of their school into the angry brown eddies. Was it all over? How could they continue? But Glen remembered God's promise. There was still something for him here. Frantically, Glen and others worked to retrieve what they could from the swift, swollen river before the water swept it away to the sea.

Drenched and exhausted, the students and staff gathered on the muddy, new bank of a vastly widened river. Charla stood with them. She had just forded the river by allowing two men to tie her to a rope and pull her across. She came to deliver a pouch of much-needed cash to help the mission survive the following weeks of isolation due to washed-out roads and bridges. Now she faced the circle of discouraged and weary faces.

"The Bible school is not going to close," she stated firmly.

Glen could not believe his ears. When she finished speaking, he went straight to her. "Sister Charla," he asked, a pleading urgency in his voice, "are you for real? Did you really mean that?"

"I certainly did," she smiled.

"How will you do it?"

"I don't know," Charla said with more calm than she felt, "but God will show us."

God did show them, and miraculously, classes resumed the following week. Still, Glen wondered what more God had for him in Mexico. School did not come easily. The pressure grew intense as he struggled to overcome his inability to read and write as well as the others. Often, he felt like it was all a hopeless waste of time.

Glen wasn't the only one feeling the frustration. After the flood, the board drafted Minerva Trujillo out of the mission office and into the position of reluctant Bible school administrator and teacher. Minnie, an experienced schoolteacher from Mexico City, had her hands full with both Raul Garcia and Glen in the same class.

One day, Minnie returned a composition to Glen with the following instructions. "Please rewrite this and add punctuation and capital letters." Glen dutifully rewrote the paper, exactly the same way. But at the end, just as instructed, he added a row of punctuation marks – periods, commas, exclamation points and question marks. After that, he wrote out a row of capital letters. He returned the paper with the attached note, "Dear Teacher, please put these where they belong. If you have any left over, give me a call."

Poor Minerva ran to see Dr. Luc, exploding with exasperation. "How am I supposed to teach these burros?!"

Despite the doubts of many, Charla and Corrine Ehrick both knew God had His hand on Glen and believed in his calling. With much loving and prayerful support from these two spiritual mothers, Glen graduated in the spring of 1995. He notes, "It was the first time I had completed anything – other than a jail sentence – in my life."

As a Bible school student, Glen helped out as a youth leader in one of the satellite churches in the tiny, neighboring town of Chula Vista. In Chula Vista, he discovered what God had for him in Mexico. Her name was Rosa.

Glen remembers, "For three years I had prayed for a wife. I asked for a girl to be with me in good times and bad ... who would pray for me, encourage me, speak the truth to me ... I also asked for a wife who could preach and teach." Rosa, a native Mixteca, has also graduated from the mission Bible school and ministers effectively among her own people in the area.

Glen accepted a position with the mission's outreach division and the newlyweds began their life together – in a donated, converted bus. In 1996, Glen and Rosa used a $1,000 wedding gift to buy a piece of property for their ministry. The couple deeded this land to the mission and began to build a new drug rehabilitation center on it. Although it started as a pegboard shanty, the rehab center is now a beautiful block home that houses twelve to eighteen men at a time. Bible studies at the rehab center became so popular with the surrounding townspeople that a church had to be built. In time, a crew from the Valley Vineyard in Reseda, California helped to build a home for Glen, Rosa and their two children.

Today, Glen pastors this growing church and still manages to serve as director at the rehab center and as supervisor of outreach for the mission.

God's redemptive power has reached into every area of Glen's life. Three brothers have come to the Lord through Glen's testimony and gone to Bible school, including Luis who is now a preacher!

In 1999, God restored another broken piece of Glen's life. Glen often thought about his father and longed to know him. God spoke to Rosa, telling her Glen's father was still alive, but no one knew how to find him. At that time, Glen and Rosa decided to fly to Oaxaca to visit a young man from the rehab center and encourage him in his new ministry. Instead, a couple of mission volunteers, Burl and Audrey Carter, offered to drive them. Passing through Casa Grandes, Chihuahua, Glen remembered he had relatives there and asked if they could take a little detour to ask around.

To Glen's mounting excitement, they met relatives who thought his father, Luis, lived in Tabasco, Zacatecas. Once they got to Tabasco however, Glen's heart sank. There were over a million and a half people in this city and they had no address! As Burl maneuvered the wide motor home through impossibly narrow streets, Glen glanced out at the bustling crowds.

"Stop!" Glen yelled, hardly believing what he saw.

Before Burl could park the vehicle, Glen was out and running to a man he had seen sitting in the shade of a tree. Glen remembers, "It was as if he was just waiting for someone."

At first his father did not recognize him, saying, "You've mistaken me for someone else." But when Glen told him things only a son could know, his face lit up. "You **are** my son! How did you find me?"

"By a miracle of God," Glen replied.

In a very healing reunion, Glen asked his father's forgiveness for all the shame he had caused – and for the several attempts he had made on his father's life as a teenager. Grandpa Luis now comes to Baja to visit Glen, Rosa and his two new grandchildren.

Glen is looking once again for his daughter, Lourdis. After Glen first became a Christian, he enjoyed four years of a renewed relationship with this beautiful girl. Then his last letter to her came back marked, "Return to sender. No forwarding address." God knows where Lourdis is and Glen is praying for another miracle.

It's been many years since Glen's "release date" from his prison of sin and pain. Today Glen is a captive of love. He explains, "My desires are totally changed. Now I just want to serve Jesus. Wherever He goes, I want to follow. Wherever He is, that's where I want to be. I want to die still serving Him."

"Though I am free and belong to no man,
I make myself a slave to everyone,
to win as many as possible."
(1 Corinthians 9:19)

Chapter 4

Fire from Ashes

"They reeled and staggered like drunken men;
*   they were at their wits' end.*
Then they cried out to the LORD in their trouble,
*   and he brought them out of their distress.*
He stilled the storm to a whisper;
*   the waves of the sea were hushed.*
They were glad when it grew calm,
*   and he guided them to their desired haven.*
Let them give thanks to the LORD for his unfailing love
*   and his wonderful deeds for men."*
(Psalm 107:27–31)

The wiry, leather-skinned Triqui man swung the heavy sack of pineapples onto his back. The weight bent his short frame almost in half. Sweat trickled down his dusty neck and brow, met with other trickles and formed rivers that soaked his torn shirt. He tugged at the rag in his belt and mopped his face, leaving smudges of mud. At least he had work. For three years, illness had prevented him from supporting his wife Maria and seven children. Now, in the pineapple fields of Vera Cruz, he could work off the debt that had forced him to flee his home in Oaxaca.

Season followed season, crop followed crop, and Juan Merino followed them both. After the pineapples came the tomato harvest in Sinaloa. Rumors told of work in Baja, real jobs that paid good money. The family arrived in 1981 only to discover the bitter reality of more hard work and little pay.

The foreman at the flower ranch showed Juan to a long steel building, segmented into a row of fifteen family units. It stank of raw sewage and stale smoke. Untended, sickly children sat in the dirt, staring dully at the new arrivals. Juan bowed his head, silently accepting what he could not change. He had no money to take his family home.

Maria fought the despair that wrapped around her heart. They worked so hard! Still, from her marriage at thirteen, she and Juan had known nothing but poverty. When her two eldest daughters went to the fields, she felt their dreams die along with those of thousands of other nameless, hunched bodies that dotted the hot, furrowed hills. More and more, Juan and Maria looked to alcohol and their native witchcraft for escape and their home grew increasingly violent.

Shortly after arriving in Baja, their grown son Felix, came to visit from Tijuana. He seemed strangely different. He spoke with great urgency about a God named Jesus and the need to repent. He spoke of hope and a new life that could be lived through the power of this Jesus. Felix took his father to the church at the mission.

One day, Juan came home to Maria and began to plead. "We should at least listen to Felix."

"He's a Christian! We are not Christians! I don't want anything to do with that stuff," Maria retorted.

"But look at the way he has changed – and look at us. We drink and fight, drink and fight. I think I would like God to change me like Felix."

The next time Felix came, he surprised his parents with an eager request.

"Papa, I want to pray for Dominga."

Juan looked at his three-year-old daughter lying on the sheet of plywood that served as the family bed. Dominga didn't walk, the result of multiple birth defects. She knew little of life beyond her pile of ragged blankets and the smoky shadows of their tiny home. Juan hesitated. As a medicine man in Oaxaca, he had already prayed to many spirits and tried all the rituals for healing. Why hope again?

"Mama," Felix persisted, "Jesus can heal her!"

Maria shrugged. She had accepted this heartbreak long ago. Let Felix pray and see for himself how foolish he was.

Felix quietly asked Jesus to heal his little sister. The next day, for the first time, Dominga began to walk.

The day Dominga walked, Pastor David Mendez from the mission came to visit and offered the family a ride to church. At the altar call, Juan gave his heart to Jesus. Immediately, he lost all desire to drink. He discarded all the paraphernalia related to their occult rituals and superstitions. Most incredibly, for Maria, she and Juan fell in love again. At once they began to share with their neighbors what God had done. Maria recalls, "That's when I truly repented and began to pray daily, praying and fasting for my children."

After three years in the camp, Juan was offered a job in the mission orchard and given a small space at the Bible school property along the river bed where he could build a house. In the orchard, among the macadamia nut trees, Juan discovered his calling as an intercessor. He named every tree after someone he knew as a reminder, and prayed for each person as he lovingly tended the trees.

When Juan first accepted Christ, he struggled to understand his Spanish Bible. He went to Marie Morales, a volunteer from the mission who was teaching his children to read, and asked if she could find another Triqui Christian to help him in his own language. Marie wrote to the Wycliffe Institute and soon had a response from Barbara Hollenbach, a missionary with New Tribes Mission. When Barbara came to visit the Merino family, Juan was astonished to recognize her as the missionary he had seen in Oaxaca 20 years earlier! He knew her as the strange lady who sometimes passed out medicine to poor people. Often he had stopped to talk to her on the street and answer her funny questions about his language. Together, Juan and Barbara have worked to bring the Triqui New Testament to completion.

In 1995 Barbara brought a crew from the United States to dub a Triqui version of the *Jesus* film, using the voices of the Merino family. Because a written Triqui language has only recently been developed, most Triqui are unable to read their own language. Juan and others in his family have just finished recording the entire New Testament on tape. Hundreds of these tapes are being copied and distributed through evangelism teams.

Today, Juan and Maria's *eleven* children all serve the Lord in various ways. Their son Antonio, recently graduated from Bible school and supervises the mission's agricultural program. When Antonio can get away from his tasks in the orchard, he joins his parents. This family trio has a regular circuit of Triqui cell groups that they visit and disciple in surrounding towns.

Juan and Maria burn with a passionate love for Jesus. Although they are past retirement age, they make almost daily trips to the camps. They go from shack to shack, praying for the sick and sharing the love and power of Jesus. They report, "We are seeing people healed and now these people are testifying themselves!" From the ashheap of alcoholism, superstition and witchcraft, Jesus is raising up a Church on fire!

"For you know that it was not with perishable things such as silver or gold that you were redeemed from the empty way of life handed down to you from your forefathers, but with the precious blood of Christ ... "
(1 Peter 1:18–19)

PART II

Our Compassionate God

A man I don't know recently received a missionary newsletter describing conditions of overwhelming misery in a third-world country. Severe famine, rampant AIDS and the destruction of war have left tens of thousands of orphans to fend for themselves in the streets and garbage dumps of this nation. This American man's response came across my path in a forwarded email. He writes, "I actually found myself responding with familiar words: 'Where is God?' Often people say this question is pivotal in their decision against faith. The answer came to me quicker than I was comfortable with. 'Where Lloyd, are you?' After all, don't Christians claim to be God's representatives here on earth?"

We know from the Gospels that Jesus never shrank from human suffering. He went out to meet it and did something about it. Today His physical, bodily presence is gone. The Church is now called the Body of Christ, present in this world to pick up where Jesus left off. 1 John 4:17 says, *"In this way, love is made complete among us . . . because in this world we are like him."*

Here are stories of just a few of the many who have risen to that calling – the calling to be the hands and feet of Jesus in this world, going where He would go and doing what He would do. They have recognized the answer to Lloyd's question. Where is God? He lives in and through those who are willing to let His compassionate heart beat within them.

Chapter 5

Jesus in the Camps

*"Go through the **camp** and tell the people,
'Get your supplies ready. Three days from now you will cross
the Jordan here to go in and take possession of the land
the LORD your God is giving you for your own.'"*
(Joshua 1:11)

Shake, rattle and roll along. Every nut and bolt of the van has the jitters. As the driver aims around each pothole ahead, the rest of the outreach team tries to talk above the racket in road-induced vibratos.

"Don't worry!" Manuel Vilar, the outreach supervisor shouts to a visitor from Canada. "If we break down, they will stop."

He points to the rear window. Another van follows but its similar condition offers no solace to the foreigners. They glance around the interior of the vehicle, exchanging silent eye-rolls while trying to remain outwardly nonchalant. They notice a coathangar where the door handle should be and a gear shift that relies heavily upon duct tape.

"This is it." Manuel points to a compound surrounded by a fence of sticks interwoven with thorn briar.

Within the enclosure, rows of corrugated tin housing stretch in grim, smoke-blackened lines across hardpacked dirt. Short, sun-weathered women gather around a communal water tap. Some carry wash buckets of laundry. Children fill plastic cups and return to their mothers who tend fires built just outside the doors of the 10' × 10' segments of tin allotted to their families.

They notice the arriving vans and most of the young ones come running. They know that Anglo visitors usually bring candy. The women are curious, but busy. The sun will go down soon, plunging the camp into total darkness and making it difficult to cook. Electrical wires lace the rooftops, but the power hasn't been on in months. They work fast.

Manuel and Abel, his assistant, jump from the van. The passenger door opens, if you know the trick, only from the outside. Abel releases the visiting team. Everyone helps to unload the equipment – movie screen, generator, video projector, a box of gospel tracts, New Testaments in Spanish, and a portable P.A. system. Men from the camp saunter over to watch. One grinning, elderly man with weepy eyes gives Manuel a bear hug. Manuel knows the man is drunk but hugs him anyway, as if he were his own father.

The visitors from Canada and Chicago look for ways to be helpful in spite of the language barrier. Some are simply trying to process the poverty before them without appearing rudely fascinated at how anyone can live in such crowded and filthy conditions. One woman turns her face to the van and mumbles through her tears, "I wouldn't let my dog live like this."

Within twenty minutes or so, no one is idle. Some members of the team begin to canvas the rows of housing, greeting the residents in a few crash-course phrases of broken Spanish, and handing out tracts. Their speaking efforts elicit everything from polite smiles to gales of mutual laughter. With gestures and what is apparently gibberish, they invite the migrant workers over to the courtyard, where a film will be shown at dusk.

Younger visitors reach into their pockets and retrieve bottles of nail polish and bubble soap, brought for the occasion. Word spreads and they are instantly surrounded by swarms of children jostling and squirming for position. Little girls hold outstretched hands, wiggling and giggling with excitement. A teenager from Calgary brandishes a bottle of Apple Red with metallic sparkles and starts a happy riot. The boys chase bubbles as they are blown into the evening breeze. Like children everywhere, these kids love to be teased, tickled and whisked about on piggyback. They blossom when touched by the slightest warm ray of genuine affection.

A little girl, maybe four years old, tugs at the skirt of a stranger, then reaches up with thin, dirt-streaked arms. The woman bends down and swings the featherweight child onto her hips.

"Como se llama?" she asks in the little Spanish she knows.

The girl smiles shyly and clings to her new friend's neck. "Anna Maria."

Anna Maria's bare feet are scabbed and bruised. Her dress is several sizes too big and hangs so long the hem is worn to shreds from dragging through the dirt. At one time, it was probably white. Her nose is runny and, the visitor briefly notes to herself, she probably has lice. The woman looks into the child's big, brown eyes and wonders, "What if you were mine?" Anna Maria smiles like the sun and suddenly she is the most beautiful child in the world. Eventually, little Anna Maria grows heavy and it hurts to hold her. But it hurts even more to put her down and walk away.

The generator roars to life and someone starts the video. This first one is for the children but the images are faded by a competing, late afternoon sun. Unfortunately, the team can't wait for it to get darker. The people here have to sleep early in order to get up before dawn. And it's cold. The children huddle together and look for any warm, welcoming lap. Already the coastal desert's icy, night wind bites through their thin, well-worn garments. The sun drops away during the film. Now that it's too dark to really see anything but the movie, more men slip quietly into the courtyard.

Abel turns on the P.A. and begins to preach. He knows what he's talking about. His family works in these fields. He knows the anger and the frustration that come with poverty when there are no exit doors. He knows the grief of watching simple illnesses turn to chronic, then deadly, disease because malnourished, overworked bodies just don't recover. He understands the desperate hope offered by spiritists and shamans, and the fleeting comfort of alcohol. The needs are many; the pain is great. Satan, the one who comes to lie, steal and destroy, has touched their lives with devastating evil. Abel preaches one answer. His name is Jesus. Abel calls for repentance from sin and invites them to the One who cared enough to come down, be one of them, and give His life for them.

The bright, halogen light behind Abel casts each raised hand into silhouette. Slowly the crowd shifts itself. Some walk away.

Some press through to the center and wait. Abel leads them in prayer and invites them to stay a bit longer to receive their own Bible. The team begins to pray for the sick.

The first man herds his entire family to the front. "Please," he mutters hoarsely, "we are all sick from the insecticides. Pray the poison will leave our bodies."

Manuel and several others lay hands on the family. Chemical poisoning from toxins is common in this area, evidenced by the high rate of cleft palates and other birth defects. A Mixteco woman in the crowd steps forward and shares a testimony of her child's healing. Now more families also want prayer for toxic poisoning.

A small cluster of young men wait, then muster up the courage to make their request. "I want to be free from my drinking," the first one blurts out. His friends nod in agreement.

"Me too," they chime in.

Manuel wraps his arm around a boy of eighteen and surprises him with his own confession. "I was a drug addict. When I turned to Jesus, He gave me the power to overcome my addiction. He will help you too."

It's late. Everyone is tired. After packing up the equipment, visitors and staff pile back into the vans for a one-hour drive back to the mission in Vicente Guerrero. By now, the visitors are missing the dinner they didn't eat because dinner is served in the dining hall at 5:00 p.m. and outreach teams leave at 4:00 p.m. Does anyone have bread and peanut butter in the dorm room?

Still, no one really cares about the hunger or the late hour. What a privilege to be just a small part of what God is doing among these people.

Abel

Abel is a local from Vicente Guerrero. He remembers the first time he came to the mission church. He had been warned all his life to stay away from Protestants but something was going on in that building down the road and he wanted to know what it was. He was eighteen, feeling brave and nosy. He came anyway and with a shock, realized he could actually *see* the love of God in people there. Six months later, he accepted Christ.

After two years God began to stir Abel's heart for evangelism. Since he had to work in the fields with his parents, he didn't know how that would ever be possible, but he began to pray with the pastor about it. Soon other Christian young men were coming to his house at night. Even though they had just worked a long day in the fields and had no car, they would walk to the camps to preach and pray for the sick.

In 1989 Abel joined the mission's first Bible school class. He remembers his favorite teacher, Jon Cowpersmith. "Jon did not just teach through his knowledge of the Word, but by the love he showed his students. Most of all, I remember the way he prayed for the Holy Spirit to touch our hearts and encouraged us to persevere in spite of struggles and trials."

Abel has been part of the outreach staff for over ten years now. Through many experiences, he has learned to trust the working of the Holy Spirit. As an example, he tells about a recent experience at Campo Cabellos.

Abel had been here before. He knew the crowd. Of all the camps, these people were the most steeped in witchcraft and the most hostile to the gospel.

Perhaps out of boredom or curiosity, the crowd huddled in front of the folding table that served as a speaker's platform. The karaoke mic was turned up full blast and Abel began to preach on repentance. Suddenly, his voice failed. Nothing. Not even a hoarse whisper. He stopped, wondering what to do. The next moment, an intense awareness of God's presence fell upon him and he began to cry. The team of visitors from Valley Vineyard of Reseda began to cry too.

No one said another word. Gradually, in the silent darkness, figures began to move forward. More and more sounds of weeping rippled through the crowd as people began to repent and ask for deliverance from demonic bondage. That night, without human voice, the Holy Spirit spoke to the deepest places of the heart.

On another occasion, a man at Campo Maclovio Rojas came to Abel desperately asking for someone to pray for his very sick wife. Abel and Juan Merino (see Chapter 4) went to the home and immediately felt a heavy, demonic oppression. The wife began to scream in pain, "I'm burning! I'm burning!" Her husband explained that this happened often. He had taken her to the government clinic, but doctors could find nothing physically wrong with her. In addition, no one could explain the bruises that covered her body.

When they found out she was going to a witch doctor for healing, Abel and Juan began to pray and fast for her. At first she was hostile to their visits and didn't want them to come. The husband persisted and she gradually began to respond as they shared the love of God. One day, during a visit, another man came into the house. Abel didn't know who he was but continued talking.

"Sister, only God can heal you. You must put your faith solely in Jesus and stop going to the witch doctor."

Turning to the strange man, Abel invited him to put his faith in Jesus as well. The man walked quickly out of the house. Then, Abel and Juan went out and prayed over the house and yard, asking for protection from all demonic curses.

The next week, they found a completely transformed woman. She met them with a broad, radiant smile.

"I'm free! I'm not sick anymore! I have Jesus in my heart." Then she added with a laugh. "You know that man who was in my house? He's the witch doctor! He never came back."

Abel remembered his words, warning the woman to stay away from witch doctors. They all roared with laughter.

Today, this dear lady is often seen at church. Her once-emaciated frame is back to a healthy weight and she glows with love for Jesus – the One who sets the prisoner free.

Manuel

Manuel, the mission's outreach supervisor, looked at Jon Cowpersmith, the elderly missionary and teacher. What now? The man on the hospital bed was dead. They had prayed, but God did not heal. The doctor sighed and tried to comfort the two ministers with a feeble pat on their backs.

"Thank you for coming. Do you want to notify the family, or shall we?"

Jon and Manuel didn't move. Something kept them rooted to the bedside. "We're going to keep praying," Jon finally said. The doctor glanced at the nurses who had gathered to attend to the body. They smothered their surprise by finding reasons to quickly leave the room. The doctor's sympathy gave way to slight irritation.

"Fine. Take your time and say your goodbyes."

"No," Jon corrected. "We're going to pray for his life."

The doctor did not want to argue with men who were so mentally distraught they had obviously lost touch with reality. He left.

Thirty minutes later, the dead man revived. The hospital was in uproar! The man sat up and began to speak with great passion. As family, friends and staff crowded his room, he told them of seeing Jesus, heaven and hell. After sharing his amazing experience, the man slipped back into a coma, where he remains as of this writing. Ten nurses gave their lives to Christ that day, praising God for His mercy in sending this man back to testify of the unseen and eternal world.

In the past four years, Manuel has seen the miraculous many times, particularly in the migrant worker camps. "Two weeks ago," he says, "a deaf man was completely healed. Last week, a lady came in great pain with a severely distended stomach. As we prayed, her stomach went down and the pain left her."

Manuel grins. Although he never loses his sense of reverent awe, this is "normal." Miracles are simply the normal behavior of a loving God who responds to those who cry out to Him and who humbly recognize their desperate need for His touch. As a former drug addict, Manuel understands how the power of God can penetrate and transform even the most hopeless situation.

Manuel was the privileged child of a wealthy family in Spain. But when his father died, the fifteen-year-old boy found no comfort in the things that surrounded him. That tragedy, coupled with financial means, plummeted Manuel into severe drug addiction. After twelve years of rebuffing his family's pleas for him to get help, Manuel received a letter from an old friend. The friend had become a Christian and invited Manuel to come to the rehab center where he lived.

Until he arrived at that center in a far-off town, Manuel had never heard the gospel, talked of God, or even seen a Bible. He finally admitted to his friend, "I'm sorry, but this stuff about Jesus is really hard to believe." The friend continued to care for Manuel, spending a lot of time with him and praying for him. Manuel finally softened – a little. "I'm going to watch you every day," he told his friend, "and see if what you talk about is real." After three months, Manuel could no longer resist the love he saw in his friend's life. "What you have, I want," he told him.

God answered that prayer, filling Manuel with a deep and practical love for the hurting and struggling. After graduating from Bible school in Sevilla, Manuel served for four years at a rehab center in Brooklyn, New York with Bethel Ministries. In New York, he fell in love with Elba, an exuberantly cheerful dentist from Mexicali who soon left to join the FFHM mission in Baja. It didn't take much persuading to get Manuel to follow! The couple married in February of 1999 and Manuel soon accepted the position of outreach supervisor.

Each Monday, the outreach team gathers to pray for guidance in the coming week. Which camps should they visit? Where is Jesus asking them to go? "The key," Manuel says, "is relying on the Holy Spirit and not just making a program."

"This is a time of great harvest," Manuel explains. "We are reaping what was sown by people like Charla who gave their lives here." It's obvious that Manuel loves his job. "I get to share the gospel and see people come to Jesus. Every night is a new experience and every night is the best night!"

John 1:14 says that, *"The Word became flesh and dwelt among us."* Literally translated, he "pitched his tent" right in our midst, in the camp of lost humanity. In the Baja, we see literal camps filled with indescribable suffering and need. Jesus continues to come into the midst of His people, manifesting His love, His presence and power through those who carry His Spirit within them.

"The Word became flesh and made his dwelling among us.
We have seen his glory, the glory of the One and Only,
who came from the Father, full of grace and truth."
(John 1:14)

Chapter 6

A Teacher's Choice

"When Jesus landed and saw a large crowd,
*he had **compassion on them**, because they were like sheep*
without a shepherd. So he began teaching them many things."
(Mark 6:34)

The college girl from Long Beach, California silently rehearsed her classroom Spanish, mentally going over the phrases she would probably need for the seven-hour bus ride from Tijuana to the tiny town of Colonia Vicente Guerrero. She had been coming for three years now, four to five times a year, devoting most every holiday and school break to a pack of exuberant, Mexican orphans.

The trip seemed longer than usual this time. The bus wound slowly through the hills just south of Ensenada, belching diesel from the back and inhaling black clouds of exhaust from the heavily loaded trucks that creaked along in front of them. By the time they reached the coastal flatland, she welcomed the fresh air, dust and all, that blew through the open windows.

The bus dropped her off along the interstate highway, the only paved road through town. From there, she walked the last half-mile to the mission. Word of her arrival spread quickly and children came running, scrambling to shower "Hermana Maria" with tight, squeezing hugs and a rain of kisses. Little brown hands reached for any part of her arms or skirt they could grab hold of. They caressed her hair and clamored for her attention. Maria was back!

Marie barely had one foot in the door before the housemother headed out, leaving her in charge of 30 little girls. Marie recalls, "I wasn't really used to all the hugging. I was training to be a teacher, but it was the kids here who taught me to show love and affection."

In those days, four adults cared for around 50–60 children. One couple cared for the boys, a single woman cared for the girls and another woman cared for the toddlers. Visitors were rare, but when they did come, they gave the staff some much-needed rest.

This time Kay Lawrence, the mission administrator's wife, filled Marie in on the task awaiting her. "Felicia is sick. Viviana's mother was supposed to visit but never showed up. She's been crying all day and won't talk to anyone. I'm so glad you're here."

Marie dropped her backpack on the kitchen table, briefly noting how much the plastic-laminate tabletop had cracked and peeled since her last visit. It felt good to be needed, but a nap would feel even better – at least at that moment.

In 1980, like thousands of other young university graduates from the Land of Opportunity, Marie considered her future. Any one near the border could see that the tide of human ambition flowed northward, not southward to the desolate Baja desert. Could she leave everything behind? And if she did, would the sacrifice be worth it – just to help a few children? Yet, didn't Jesus leave everything to cross the cosmos and reach a relative handful of people in another dry, dusty corner of the world?

During the next three years, Marie taught kindergarten at the mission, married a Mexican national and had her first baby. But something else caught her attention. The children at the mission went to school, and the Mexican children in town went to school – but the poorest ones, the children of the migrant farm workers, were either left at home or taken to the fields. Excluded by poverty and prejudice, it was impossible for these kids to enroll in school. They lived in cardboard shanty settlements and certainly had no money for the required uniforms, shoes or books. Schools demanded birth certificates and these families, mostly from the primitive mountains of Oaxaca, had no such documentation. The local caste mentality stifled any efforts to change the rules.

Marie found her cause. Going to the mission board, she asked for the use of a Sunday school room for three months. She developed her own literacy materials and began to drive her pick-up truck, with her baby on the seat beside her, from settlement to settlement, picking up children who wanted to learn.

That summer, Marie started with twenty-three children of all ages who had never been in a classroom and never been confined to a desk. One little girl, possibly six years old, was Margarita. She had only one dress, yellow and torn from hem to waist on both sides. Each day she sat with her hands firmly clenched around fistfuls of her yellow dress, not daring to move. No matter what, she was going to read!

At the end of the three months, seventeen children read at a second grade level. One of the little boys was Antonio Merino, now the head of the mission's agricultural program. Largely through Marie's literacy class, Antonio's ten siblings all came to Christ.

But seventeen children learning to read was not enough. Those seventeen needed to continue in school. And what about the hundreds of others for whom the door to education remained closed? Marie refused to accept the status quo. Mary Solario, one of the mission staff, had a relative who happened to be the "delegado," the head of all local government. Marie traveled to Ensenada and pleaded for his help. In an amazing act of mercy, he helped Marie produce the required documents. He entered the names of all seventeen children into a book of birth records, guessing at their ages and assigning birth dates on the spot. Gifts from donors provided the necessary books, uniforms and supplies. Marie helped illiterate parents with registration and forms.

Those early efforts of one stubborn, young teacher from Long Beach began a gradual change in the climate. Today, a local education office, better informed parents, and new child labor laws (though often ignored) make things a bit easier. There is at least a ray of hope for all the children of Baja, regardless of social standing.

Marie's truck bounced through hard-packed ruts, the only vestige of a road across the featureless, brown hills. Her toddler, Rosalee, nestled against the new baby, Anna.

Occasionally the neat, prickly rows of a cactus plot, surrounded by a feeble hint of fencing, broke up the monotony. A few unfinished, cinderblock houses appeared in the shimmering heat. With bony fingers of re-bar poking out the four corners of their tops, they looked a bit like the upturned cows that had died in the drought, their stiff legs stabbing at the sky.

Marie watched for the hillside covered in shrines to the dead. Turn here. Decorated with rosaries, fading icons and plastic flowers, the memorials splashed the dull hillside with tired color, like costume jewelry on an old woman.

The truck pulled into the field workers' camp – rows of makeshift homes built out of plastic garbage bags, grape vines, cardboard, anything that could be scavenged from the wasteland of the poor. Marie climbed out. She would need permission from the manager. That done, she spread her tarp alongside the truck where she could keep an eye on her sleeping baby. A cloud of children instantly materialized around the truck, buzzing and flitting like startled bees. Rosalee scampered from the seat and disappeared into the humming swarm.

For four years, Marie took the gospel to the children of five different camps – a different one each weekday afternoon. They gathered on rocks and planks, or just sat in the dirt, waiting for the lady who came with Bible stories, songs and crafts. Small gifts – a pencil, a piece of candy – brought rare pleasure to their grim lives.

When Marie had her third child, she "retired" from her work until all three were old enough to be in school. Today she is teaching at the mission's school. Inspired by Marie's early pioneer efforts, many teams from the Child Evangelism ministry now go regularly to the camps. Each week, over one thousand children are being taught, discipled and given a cup of milk and a scoop of peanut butter in Jesus' name.

Twenty-four years have passed since a bewildered college girl stepped off a bus at the edge of the Baja desert. To some, her decision to stay seemed like a foolish waste of education and opportunity, a waste of life. Was it? Jesus said, *"I tell you the truth, unless a grain of wheat falls to the ground and dies, it remains only a single seed. But if it dies, it produces many seeds."*

Because of the transient life of field workers, Marie rarely knew the children she taught for very long. It was easy for her to wonder about the fruit of her labors. One day, many years later, a young man approached her on a public bus.

"Do you remember me?" he asked.

Marie fumbled through her memory. "No, I'm sorry. I don't."

"I was a kid in one of the camps. You were my teacher."

"Really?" Marie tried to place his long-forgotten face.

"Yeah." He smiled broadly. "I'm an assistant pastor now." The bus reached his stop. He paused on the steps. "Thank you."

"I tell you the truth, unless a grain of wheat falls
to the ground and dies, it remains only a single seed.
But if it dies, it produces many seeds."
(John 12:24)

Chapter 7

Heart of the Father

*"In the same way your Father in heaven is not willing
that any of these little ones should be lost."*
(Matthew 18:14)

The horn blasted from Papa Juan's dirt-caked pick-up out front. Cuco jumped up, instantly forgetting about his imminent conquest of Manuel's choice aggies and steelies. That sound could only mean one thing. Time for clamming at the beach – and a trip to Grandma's for tacos! Leaving their marbles in the dust, the boys scrambled for choice seats. If you got a good spot on the side rails, the dry, desert wind would blow through your hair and cool your sun-baked body as the truck bounced for six miles to the neighboring town of Camalu, then turned west for another two miles to the ocean.

Papa Juan towered over the boys. He was a tall, rugged man with a hearty laugh and husky voice. Cuco adored him. Cuco had not seen his own father since being left here at the mission two years ago.

"Get in!" Juan roared. "Grandma's waiting for you!"

The twenty-four boys in Juan's care smashed and jammed themselves into impossible positions, until everyone could say, with some license, that they were "in". They took off with whoops of delight drowning out the roar of the muffler-less engine.

Juan Carillo had returned to Mexico in 1968, after coming to Christ in Fresno, California. When the mission's directors recruited him in 1973, Juan knew God was calling him to share in his heavenly Father's nature – to be a father to the fatherless.

Many children came to the orphanage with no prior education and no documentation. Juan spent much of his time battling for the rights of children as he met with school and government officials. "They had no one to protect them, no one they could turn to," he recalls.

Juan had a gift for loving children who were difficult to love. Juan Tomas was just such a boy.

By sixteen, this orphan had managed to alienate and exasperate every adult in his life. He stormed through life with an aggressive hostility that left a trail of debris in his wake. Like the rest of the older children at that time, Tomas attended the Catholic school in town. At first, the school reported the torn-down basketball hoop. Then the broken windows. Finally, when a nun tried to reprimand Tomas, the boy insolently bounced a basketball into her face and broke her glasses even as she was speaking. As far as Dave Taylor, the president of the mission board, was concerned, that was the last straw. Along with the rest of the staff, he wanted Tomas out.

Juan begged Dave for one more chance with the boy. "I'll be responsible. If there's more trouble, I'll find another place for him."

Juan took the boy back to school where Tomas asked the nun for forgiveness. Graciously, the nun hugged him but held her disciplinary ground. "Your punishment will be that you cannot go to school here."

Juan's heart sank. What was he going to do with this boy? Having accepted full responsibility for him, Juan had to keep the boy with him night and day. Fortunately, he had one more ally to share the load – Grace Roberts, a Methodist pastor's widow who served as a teacher for English-speaking children at the mission. Grace poured her time and affection into Tomas' broken life, becoming the mother he never had. Each week she invited him for dinner in her small trailer. When Tomas dreamed of buying a bicycle, she hired him for odd jobs and yard work so he could earn the money. Both Juan and Grace wept for joy when the shiny, new bike arrived and they saw Tomas' face light up with pride and glee.

Desperate to get the boy back in school, Juan decided to try at Cardenas, another small town several miles down the highway. There he pleaded Tomas' case and persuaded the staff to give the boy another chance. Tomas redeemed his chance, finishing high school and going on to study in Tijuana.

One day, Juan Carillo received a letter. Tomas had met the girl he wanted to marry. The problem was, she came from a wealthy family that considered an orphan like Tomas far beneath their social standing. The letter asked Papa Juan if he would please receive the girl's mother for a formal visit and speak to her about marriage on Tomas' behalf.

On the appointed day, the girl, her mother and uncle showed up in Camalu. The Carillo house sparkled. Tile floors were polished, new curtains graced the windows and fresh paint brightened the walls. Tomas entered, stunned at the work Juan and Elisa had gone to. The mother's cool and skeptical demeanor evaporated as they continued to visit. Finally, the subject of marriage was brought up. Tomas held his breath.

"Tomas, you told me you had no family," the girl's mother said with astonishment. "That's not true. You have the most beautiful family I've ever met!"

Today, Juan Carillo still receives letters from a grateful, grown-up Tomas. He works as an accountant in Tijuana, where he lives with his wife and children.

By 1980, a beautiful new facility at the mission was completed and the orphanage was restructured. Instead of living in dormitory-style housing that separated the boys and girls, the children now lived in family units. Each "family" consisted of twelve to fourteen children, boys and girls, housed with a married couple. Juan and Elisa parented numerous children in this manner for several years. Then in 1986, they left for another challenge – to be houseparents at the Tijuana house, a home for children of the mission who have grown up and want to pursue higher education or vocational training.

In 1997, while still at the T.J. house, Elisa died of a sudden heart attack. Juan returned to Vicente Guerrero. Before long, he was back at work, helping in the kitchen and ministering in the migrant camps with the outreach team. After almost 30 years of service, Juan just recently retired and lives near the mission with his new wife, Marta. Marta continues to work in the mission nursery. She is the older sister of Raquel, the little girl in Chapter 20.

Juan still keeps a list of every child ever brought into his home. Except for a few that disappeared after leaving the mission, Juan remains in contact with each one. He writes, he visits, they often visit him, he prays for them daily. Juan is just one of many men who have come to the mission and embraced the children. The Spirit of God lives in these men as they nurture, protect, guide and bless. To children who have broken and distorted images of what a "father" is, God uses Juan and others to reveal Himself – a Father to the fatherless.

" 'My son,' the father said, 'you are always with me,
and everything I have is yours."
(Luke 15:31)

Chapter 8

The Gift of Family

"He came and preached peace to you who were far away
and peace to those who were near. For through him
we both have access to the Father by one Spirit.
Consequently, you are no longer foreigners and aliens,
but fellow-citizens with God's people and
members of God's household ... "
(Ephesians 2:17–19)

It's Wednesday – dump day at the mission. Mike and Marsha VanAmburgh are making dozens of sandwiches in their small kitchen. They fill recycled water bottles and milk cartons with safe well water from the tap. A group of visitors from Park Community Church in Chicago is gathering at the warehouse where they will meet before heading to the "basura" (garbage dump).

A driver navigates the flatbed truck and trailer across the crowded mission lot and several visitors jump on. As they stop at various trash depots on the property, the volunteers load on a dozen 55-gallon barrels of this week's garbage. They will have more to deliver than the mission's waste, however. Two vans follow the truck, carrying duffel bags that the visitors have packed with tarps, soap, oil, towels, and a load of socks and shoes.

Soon the vehicles are raising clouds of dust that signal their arrival at the rotting, smoldering sea of trash. The scavengers seem to rise up from nowhere. From a distance they are invisible;

their hunched bodies blend discreetly into the mottled wasteland around them. As the truck approaches, they straighten their backs and quickly converge on the newly arriving possibilities.

The 55-gallon trash barrels are overturned off the truck and garbage spills everywhere. Barefoot children in filthy rags vie for position so they can be the first to find a scrap of uneaten bread or a baggie of someone's expired leftovers. They stab through everything with their sticks, tearing apart boxes and bags. With unrestrained hunger, they skewer tin cans and peer hopefully inside for overlooked remains. It's hard to watch. Some of the visitors turn away, trying to hide their uncontrollable tears.

After the initial shock of seeing such stark poverty, the visitors get organized. They spread blue plastic tarps over broken glass, jagged tin and vermin-infested ground. They fill basins with water and arm themselves with weapons of mercy – weapons designed to beat back the pain and despair the Enemy has wreaked on these lives. Today, 150 of Guerrero's most destitute have gathered around the truck.

The tarps quickly fill with children, some rowdy and eager, some quiet and shy. The team members tenderly bathe each child's feet and hands. Cuts and burns are treated with ointment and wrapped. Each one is anointed with oil and prayed for. Socks and shoes emerge from the van and end up on just the right feet! Everyone receives a sandwich and a drink of clean water.

One American woman gets a bit testy when the poor around her begin to grab for more. "Why are they being so selfish and unfair" she wonders, "when others are still waiting?" Suddenly she remembers the designer sunglasses on her head and feels instantly shamed. She knows her glasses cost more than everything the lady before her is trying to take. Who is she to talk about what is fair?

Love connects. By the end of the day, sounds of laughter and joyful playing fill the air. Each one, whatever their language or country, has been touched by the hand of God.

Mike and Marsha VanAmburgh lead the dump ministry, carrying on a work started by Anne and Ernie Stahl, a retired couple who visited the mission periodically for many years. Many of those who live around the dump now consider Mike and Marsha more than just friends; they are family. But then, Mike and Marsha have always had the gift of creating "family".

It was 1974. A sizzling Iranian sun flashed and danced off the rippling water of the Sena Hotel pool in Tehran. Marsha Beauchamp, a young American teenager, tried to keep her pale, white skin in the shifting shade of the umbrella. Her father, an oil refinery engineer, worked for Iranian civilian interests. Marsha noticed a young man in United States Air Force tans squinting her way. The hand cupped over his eyes trailed a wisp of cigarette smoke. He caught her glance and took it as a bit of encouragement. As he approached her lounge chair, she registered a more complete first impression. Beer in his other hand. Soldier boy. No thanks.

Mike gave it his best shot but barely had the words out of his mouth before Marsha stopped him cold.

"Look, I'm a Christian," she said, her eyes resting on his beer can, "and I'm just not interested."

For Americans, Tehran was a small place. The two couldn't help but continue to bump into each other. Mike persisted. Finally, Marsha acquiesced to a "missionary date". She would go out with him if he would go to church with her. Agreed.

"After all," Mike reasoned, "it probably won't kill me."

Little did he expect it to give him a new life. Mike had never heard the gospel. Because his parents had not been able to agree on a religion, he had grown up without attending any church at all. The message hit him like a well-placed bomb.

"I didn't need to hear it twice. I knew where I was going!" he explains.

For the next several months, Mike read the Gospels of Matthew and John over and over. He bought a complete Bible and continued to study after being transferred to Greece, away from Marsha. Later, back in New York, his heart and thoughts returned to the young girl he had met under the desert sun. Marsha was attending college in California now. Mike headed west and married her.

Very quickly, Mike felt drawn to missions. When his pastor saw a passion in Mike for ministering to others, he arranged for a test that got Mike into Multnomah Bible College in Oregon.

Mike and Marsha didn't go far to find their mission field. They began to work in their own backyard – inner-city Portland – through a ministry called World Impact. Although they had four children of their own by now, they could not turn away from the hurting hearts and broken lives they found in the ghettos, discarded like so much litter. When a drug-addicted mother in the streets abandoned her son, they took him in. When an ambitious attorney decided her career was more important than her children, they took her three out-of-control boys in too. Soon their family swelled to ten.

On an errand to pick up more New Testaments for their street ministry, Mike went to the printers, Christian Literature International, in Canby, Oregon. That errand redirected their lives. CLI's printer had just gone, leaving CLI in crisis. Mike had worked a bit in a print shop during high school and now felt God speaking to his heart.

"Well," he said, half jokingly, "if you don't mind me wasting some paper, I'll come out and learn how to run the press and print for you."

"We can't afford to pay you," the man quickly warned.

"That's OK. If the Lord wants us here, He'll provide," Mike responded. For the next seventeen years, God provided!

Mike and Marsha moved to Canby with no money, but knew God had something for them there. Through a series of amazing circumstances, they ended up living in a converted church built in 1915. They pumped out and repaired the ever-flooded basement, built loft rooms under the eaves, and planted a small "farm". Their growing family expanded again as they began to care for young women through a crisis pregnancy ministry. Mike would come home, from time to time, with children from the streets. Usually, some derelict parent had begged him to take their child and provide a home.

One day, Mike remarked to Marsha, "We should go into orphanage work."

Marsha stared in disbelief. "We *have* an orphanage!"

Ask them today how many children they have raised and they both laugh. They've lost count.

"About 29 ... I think." Mike grins, "I always felt like I wanted to work with children."

What about Marsha?

"I never asked!" Mike admits.

Marsha just smiles with the infinite patience of a mother who has borne ten of her own offspring.

The VanAmburghs finally became officially licensed foster parents when they took in Nathaniel, a boy with cerebral palsy. Josh, their tenth and last son by birth, had also been born with the crippling disease. God, Who sees the end from the beginning, used this time to give Marsha the special training and experience she would draw upon many years later. Working with her sons, and as a volunteer in the school system, Marsha discovered her wonderful gifting as a therapist's assistant for the handicapped.

The VanAmburghs sold their unique home to a daycare center and, after 24 years with CLI, Mike finally took a "paying job" with a commercial printer in Silverton. Two years later, he realized that ministry still tugged at his heart. He had a good salary, but no satisfaction.

Mike didn't know it yet, but God was about to use all their years of experience in a new ministry, a new country, a new life! Their home church, Bethany Evangelical Free in Canby, had a connection to FFHM and was sending a team to build a septic tank for the new children's center in Oaxaca. Mike signed on to go. By the time he returned, he was hopelessly in love with the dark-eyed, dusky children of Mexico. But Marsha had little enthusiasm for going anywhere and leaving behind their fourteen grandchildren, so Mike prayed.

"God, I think you're calling me to Mexico, but I'm not going unless you speak to her, too."

Marsha recalls this period. "I was dry, spiritually wiped out. I was struggling with my teenagers, bitter and mad at God. One day, I was watching the Matthew videos and suddenly, God revealed Jesus to me. Not the way I had always thought of Him, but the way I needed to see Him as a man of joy. Joy is what I desperately needed at this time. I experienced total renewal in one miraculous moment! I was free!"

Marsha began to wonder why God had given her this extraordinary experience. Was He leading her somewhere? Preparing her for a new ministry? Obviously, God knew how badly she had needed this, but for what purpose?

As she tested out the waters in various areas, nothing seemed right. Finally, she realized God was telling her to submit to Mike's leading. "OK," she announced, "I'm ready to go to Mexico."

Mike applied with FFHM, but had no idea what services he could offer that they needed. He also doubted if FFHM would accept a couple of their age with a severely handicapped child.

Mike still sounds shocked. "FFHM accepted our application and all the baggage that came with us!"

When they came to the Baja mission in May of 2000, Mike was surprised to learn that the printer, Ken Grassman, was also from Canby and had been praying for his replacement. Ken was sure Mike had been dropped from heaven! Charla had a surprise as well when she recognized Mike. Long ago, on one of her many speaking trips, a friend had taken her to see CLI's printshop. Who would have guessed the man she met that day would be the printer at the mission twenty years later?

Marsha bonded instantly with Angel Silva and began to help with the wheelchair ministry. She brings a compassionate mother's understanding to the work of helping the handicapped. And since old habits are hard to break, the VanAmburghs continue to open their home, caring for babies that come to the clinic in critical condition. Each child has touched them in a profound way, expanding their hearts as well as their household. Brenda, an abandoned child, is one such treasure they've taken to raise as their own.

Because Brenda suffered from cerebral palsy, her mother had allowed a boyfriend to convince her that Brenda was a waste of time and food. By the time neighbors found Brenda and brought her to the mission, the three-year-old girl had been neglected to the point of near death. Brenda is now a thriving, sparkling five-year-old. Each day she gains strength to maneuver her braced legs and walker. With every small success, she flashes a smile to melt glaciers.

The VanAmburgh's son Josh, requires frequent medical attention in San Diego to control his recurring seizures. No one knows how much longer God will allow this family to stay in Mexico. But whatever lies ahead for them, the mission has already been greatly blessed. Through them, we have truly seen the heart of the Father. We have seen the love of Jesus, whose sacrifice enables us to be "adopted as sons" and "members of God's household". Mike and Marsha have shown us the divine gift of creating family.

*"Both the one who makes men holy and those who are made holy
are of the same **family**. So Jesus is not ashamed
to call them brothers."*
(Hebrews 2:11)

Chuck and Charla Pereau

*(Chapter 1): Raul Garcia and his wife, Flor,
with some of the orphanage children in their care.*

*(Chapter 2): Alma Angulo shows visitors a millstone and sign
enscripted with Matthew 18:6 – a sober warning
to all who enter the orphanage.*

*(Chapter 3): Glen Almeraz with Charla Pereau
in front of his first church made entirely of donated French doors
and lovingly dubbed "Crystal Cathedral II."*

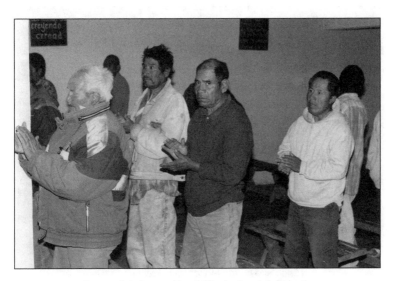

Farmers join in worship at Glen's church in Zapata.

Glen's wife, Rosa, spent many years working in the fields. She now ministers with Glen in the migrant camps.

(Chapter 5): Manuel (far left), Abel (far right) and members of outreach team in the clothing warehouse.

Visiting teams minister in the camp by providing a meal before showing the Jesus film.

(Chapter 6): Marie Morales, one of the mission's early pioneers and a dedicated teacher.

(Chapter 7): Juan Carillo, who has been a father to so many, helps a boy with the microphone so he can give thanks in the mission dining hall.

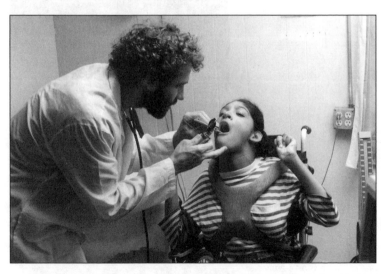

(Chapter 10): Dr. Luc Chaussé treats Sandra, Mario Cordoba's daughter who suffers from cerebral palsy.

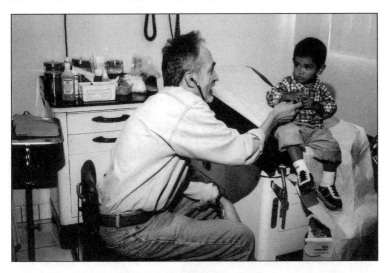

God cares for His children through volunteers like Dr. Arnie Gorske, a retired U.S. Navy doctor who visits the mission each month.

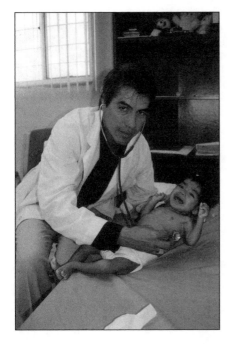

Dr. Ramon Avitia treats one of the many children who are lined up at the mission's free clinic each morning.

(Left to right): Jon Cowpersmith, Chuck Mills, Glen Almeraz and Dr. Marco Angulo break ground on the new drug rehabilitation center.

(Chapter 11): Barry Wineroth of YWAM has brought thousands of volunteers to serve the needy in the name of Jesus over the past 20 years.

So many come and help with Jesus' servant heart.
These ladies help Marian Vaine (far right) in the macademia nut kitchen.

(Chapter 12): Mario and Graciella Cordoba (on right) pray with
Jose and Cinthya Alfredo, graduates of the Bible school in Baja
who have returned to minister in their native Oaxaca.

(Chapter 13): Pastors' conference in Tlacolula, Oaxaca.

(Chapter 14): John Moore, gifted agronomist, grafts a tree in the mission orchard.

(Chapter 15): Corrine Ehrick visits with Victoria.

(Chapter 16): Jon and Eleanor Cowpersmith,
tireless veterans of the war for the souls of men.

(Chapter 17): Eva Shaffino, giving love wherever it's needed.

(Chapter 18): Pilot Joe Vaine and his wife, Marian.
Flying for Jesus *provides medical and evangelistic outreach to remote areas as well as emergency medical evacuations.*

Joe and Dr. Avitia pray with a fisherman from Santa Rosalillita to receive Christ during medical outreach visit.

(Chapter 19): Angel, a three-year-old orphan rescued from the dump, underwent many surgeries to straighten his spine.

Today Angel works with friends like Dirk and Mary Kos (on left) to minister to the handicapped of Baja.

(Chapter 20): Araceli Mejia grew up at the orphanage, then stayed as a housemother for ten years, touching many with the love of God. She still works in the mission kitchen.

(Chapter 20): Raquel, left at the mission by a single mother who could not care for her, still radiates the joy of the Lord.

(Chapter 20): Ana Laura with husband Steve Haire and son at the Morelia center they donated out of gratitude to God for her childhood at the Baja orphanage.

Children in the new Morelia orphanage.

(Chapter 21): Maria Villa Pablo visits many families as she preaches the gospel in the mountains of Oaxaca.

Children gather in front of their makeshift hovel
to receive a bag of beans and rice from the outreach team.

The author, Linda, holds the newest member of an impoverished family.
When Alma Angulo met this family, they had no food and
had been eating only salt for days.
Local Christians have built them a house.

Mike and Marsha VanAmburgh.

Little one in the loving arms of Chuck Pereau.

Chuck and Charla at the original casino converted to a soup kitchen –
now the site of a hospitality center that houses thousands of visitors each year.

Charla and Linda in the mission
dining hall.

PART III

Our Sovereign God

Who tries to put together a jigsaw puzzle without any idea what the whole picture will look like? Without any box cover to look at and use as a guide? With a simple child's puzzle, you could do it, but what if you had thousands of tiny pieces to find and place correctly?

In 1966 Chuck and Charla envisioned a children's home – run by someone *else*. They prayed for a future revival in the area – ushered in through someone *else*. They had no box cover to look at. Never in their wildest imaginings did they foresee that God would use *them* and some day the mission's sprawling complex would house not only a children's home, but a Bible school, a clinic, an outreach warehouse, a fire station, daycare center, elementary school, teen's house, and more! Beyond that, of course, are the two additional missions in Oaxaca and Morelia, the men's rehab center, ten satellite churches and the work of Bible school graduates who have been sent back as missionaries to their homelands.

Literally thousands of "pieces" have been found by God – volunteers, staff, supporters and friends – at the right time, in the right place. Without Him, the mission would be littered with fragments, frayed and frustrated by the enormity of the challenge. Instead, God has sovereignly masterminded a cohesive whole.

In Part III, you will find stories of how God found and brought just the right missing pieces to the mission. No amount of searching, recruiting or cajoling could have resulted in the diverse, yet beautiful mosaic we see today, a holy temple *"joined together"* that *"grows and builds itself up in love, as each part does its work"* (Ephesians 2:21; 4:16).

Chapter 9

A Clinic Is Born

"The LORD said, 'I have indeed seen the misery of my people in Egypt. I have heard them crying out because of their slave drivers, and I am concerned about their suffering.'"
(Exodus 3:7)

It's the early 1980s. Charla walks down the corridor of a small hospital in San Quintin, twelve miles south of the mission in Vicente Guerrero. A short, swarthy Mexican woman stops her and pulls her into a room where a baby lies in an incubator that does not work. The woman speaks quickly in Spanish and Charla tries her best to understand. The woman insists no one has fed the baby for at least twenty-four hours. Charla asks about the baby and a nurse explains that the baby is too weak to suck and needs to be fed intravenously.

Charla stares at the nurse. "Well, why aren't you doing that?"

"We don't have a needle small enough," the nurse explains.

"Why don't you get one?"

"The closest source is Ensenada."

The hospital is poorly equipped and understaffed, isolated by bad roads and no telephone service. Ensenada lies 130 miles away; a round trip means at least eight hours through the hills at best.

"Why doesn't someone go to get a needle?" Charla asks.

"Our vehicle needs repair and is not running."

Charla tries to swallow her frustration. "You can't let this baby die for lack of a needle!"

The nurse smiles hopefully. "Why don't you take the baby to the hospital in Ensenada? We'll give you a letter saying we don't have the ability to care for it."

It turns out that the woman is not the baby's mother. The baby was abandoned and the mother unknown. With the baby lying on the seat next to her, Charla heads back mumbling, "I keep getting myself into the dumbest situations."

Stopping at Guerrero, Charla decides to bequeath the task to Chuck, due to arrive at the mission that day. (Chuck was one the first to be trained as a paramedic in the Los Angeles City Fire Department. He would know how to keep this baby alive!) At the same moment, another car pulls into the mission with a couple from the Pereau's church in North Hollywood who have never visited before, Sam and Nell Greenburg. Nell is a registered nurse. The instant Nell steps out of the car, Charla approaches her with an impassioned plea. "Please go with Chuck and get this baby to the hospital!"

Hours later, Chuck and Nell arrive in Ensenada. They are told the hospital needs seven hundred dollars before they can admit the baby.

"You have to take this baby or it will die!" Chuck, an experienced rescue worker, is devastated by the plight of this tiny life ebbing away in his hands. He is sobbing and can barely speak.

The admitting clerk, a tense woman behind a small, sliding glass window, hesitates, then refuses.

"Whatever the cost, I'll come back and pay it."

The woman looks at Nell, a tall, slender red-head. "Leave this lady with us as a guarantee you will come back."

Nell gasps. Since her arrival, she has felt like an alien on the wrong planet. "I've never been to Mexico or the mission before. My husband is down at Vicente Guerrero and I am not staying at this hospital!"

Chuck reaches into his back pocket and feels his gold retirement badge. "I'll come back and pay this baby's bill." He takes out the one thing a fireman never parts with and leaves it sitting on the counter.

The next morning, Chuck shares the story with the mission staff at devotions. They take up a sacrificial offering and raise the seven hundred dollars needed. When Chuck returns to the hospital, he finds the baby has died. The bill is six hundred and eighty-some dollars. He pays and they give him back the infant's body with his gold badge. Fighting his blinding tears, Chuck brings the baby back to the mission where she is buried that night in an unmarked grave.

The clinic

Nell Greenburg attended the grim, heart-rending burial. She tried not to let it affect her, but it did. After that, Nell decided to volunteer her services at the mission. Sam had also been touched and decided to come along with her and do carpentry work. Nell began to work in the camps, treating the sick. On one memorable occasion, she found the corpse of a man who had died of tuberculosis in his cardboard hovel. Near the body was a little girl lying on the ground in a fetal position, also dying of tuberculosis. Nell brought her back to the mission and nursed her back to wholeness.

"We've got to have a clinic here!" she declared.

"We're already stretched," Charla hesitated. But Nell insisted. They looked at four little Sunday School rooms at the rear of the chapel.

"We can have an office-waiting room, two observation rooms and a delivery room!" Nell went to work and in three weeks the mission had a clinic. The waiting room quickly proved too small so Nell had grass planted outside to make the overflow patients more comfortable. She operated the clinic for several months but soon recognized the need for a fully-fledged doctor . . .

Chapter 10

God's Mighty Men of Medicine

"Then Peter said, 'Silver or gold I do not have, but what I have I give you. In the name of Jesus Christ of Nazareth, walk.'"
(Acts 3:6)

Over the years, the need for medical staff has been the subject of perpetual and earnest prayer. In answer, God has sent a series of men, like links in a mighty chain, who have come to humbly serve those who could never pay a doctor's fee. Maybe a bag of tomatoes, a few eggs – sometimes just a grateful smile. But for these doctors, the smiles were worth it all.

Dr. Mendoza

Dr. Naftali Mendoza, a Mixteco Indian from Oaxaca, was one of the first to come. He volunteered part-time for five years, often treating fifty to seventy patients a day. Their ailments were usually the direct results of poverty – skin disease, dysentery and tuberculosis. Under Dr. Mendoza, the mission gave mothers a clean place to have their babies, reducing deaths related to childbirth.

But Dr. Mendoza could not stay. He had a poor family back in Oaxaca and a responsibility to send money back to them. As he developed his own practice in town, the clinic tried to help him by referring patients who had money to pay and by giving him surplus medical supplies from mission donations. As he began to cut back his time at the free clinic, the staff prayed for help once again.

Dr. Murphy

While the board searched for a long-term replacement, an application arrived from a doctor in Chippewa, Wisconsin. Patrick Murphy had been given a copy of *Charla's Children*. After failing to get a visa to serve God in Africa, he read the book and offered himself and his wife, Ana, to serve in Vicente Guerrero for a year. Patrick and Ana came, filled with the Spirit of God, leaders who understood the principle of servanthood. "I never once saw them express an egotistic concern," Charla notes. "I thought the world was coming to an end when that year was over and they prepared to leave. How could there be another Patrick in the whole world?"

God had an answer to that question. It came through the unlikely channel of Charla's new fax machine.

Charla stood in the FFHM office – i.e. the back bedroom of their house in North Hollywood. Keith Durkin was calling from the mission in Baja.

"Please Charla, fax us the instructions for installing this new walk-in refrigerator," he pleaded. "We don't know where to begin."

Charla eyed the new machine with great apprehension. She and electronic objects had never gotten along too well. Floods, poverty and disease, what were they? Now she faced a strange gadget and sixteen pages of instructions! "I'll try," she sighed, "but you'll have to walk me through it."

Fax machines were still new then, and she had yet to use one. But there it was, freshly installed in all its multi-buttoned, beeping glory. Carefully, she began to follow the steps that Keith dictated over the phone.

In those days, sheets of paper had to be hand-fed one at a time. Just as she began the process, an incoming fax began to roll out of the machine, the paper curling out and onto the floor, foot after foot of someone's application to the mission – all in French. Panicked, Charla asked Keith what to do about her disrupted transmission.

"Hit the redial button and start over."

Charla did just that. Sixteen pages later, she called Keith. Nothing had arrived in Mexico.

"Try again," Keith insisted.

Charla did it again. Again, nothing. Again, Keith asked her to keep trying. On and on, through the morning. Meanwhile, the French application came through a second time. Rolls of uncut, slick thermal paper wrapped around Charla's feet as her frustration mounted. She recognized the application came from a doctor. That meant it must be forwarded to the board's medical advisor, Dr. Gary Johnson in Washington. As Charla struggled to feed several feet of highly uncooperative, coiling paper into her new electronic enemy, Chuck entered from the garage.

"What should we do with the bicycle tires?" he asked innocently.

"Go away!" she roared. She glared at the application. Why was she going to all this trouble, anyway? If this person didn't speak English, how could God intend him for the mission?

That afternoon, Rev. John Lucas, a board member from Calgary, Canada, called.

"Charla?" came John's bewildered voice. "I have enough faxes from you to paper my living room walls!"

Horrified, Charla suddenly realized why Keith had never received the sixteen pages of instructions – sixteen pages sent at least five times. The number in the "redial" memory was a number called by her bookkeeper the day before!

Later in the month, the phone bill came. Charla saw a strange charge for a call to India on the same day as the fax fiasco. "We don't know *anyone* in India," she complained to the phone company. Soon, a sweet letter arrived from India – from another mission office, in fact. "We don't have a walk-in refrigerator," it explained. "When is it to arrive?"

All this to say, Charla's introduction to Dr. Patrick Murphy's replacement was less than auspicious. Even when Gary Johnson called to assure her that the new doctor's background and credentials were impeccable, Charla groaned. She simply didn't want to hear it. In her mind, Patrick was next to Jesus – truly Saint Patrick. Besides, this new guy was so ... different.

When they met, Charla's impression went from bad to worse, colored by her sorrow over Patrick's departure. Dr. Luc Chaussé was French Canadian with heavily accented English and long

hair. His bohemian family reminded Charla of hippies from the
'70s. Furthermore, he did not come with any church recommen-
dation, so she couldn't be sure of his spiritual credentials. Was he
really God's answer?

Dr. Luc

Dr. Luc Chaussé took his eyes off the dirt road long enough to
take in the church building to his right. "Oh God," he groaned
with sudden cold feet, "what am I getting myself into?"

Raised by Roman Catholic parents in Quebec, Luc had always
believed in the existence of God. The God he knew had created
the world, made known His moral laws, then left man to manage
as best he could under fear of punishment. By the time Luc
graduated from medical school in 1983, the pursuit of success,
wealth and pleasure had extinguished any compulsion to follow
this distant, impersonal Rulemaker.

Luc tells of his quest for God in the book, *Ten Quebec Doctors
Talk About God.* As he began his medical practice, Luc's intimate
contact with death, sickness and human suffering jolted him
into a period of intense questioning. He spent three years studying the religions of the world, searching for answers regarding
the reason for man's existence, the purpose of suffering, the
injustice in the world and the truth regarding God. "I found
nothing but beautiful, interesting and very philosophical writ-
ings which fed my intellectual thirst without providing any food
for my heart; nothing which could really give me hope."

One day, while reading a book on the Sermon on the Mount,
Luc realized that the actual words of Jesus had an impact on his
heart that no words *about* Jesus had ever had. "I was convinced
that Jesus was the only one who could truly bring me to God,"
he explains. That night he prayed and committed himself to
following Jesus.

During the next seven years of practice, Luc felt a spiritual
conflict growing within him. He grew acutely conscious of the
fact that, as a doctor, he could only prolong life, not save it. No
matter what he did, his patients would eventually die anyway;
then what? He knew he had discovered the answer in Christ, but
was still afraid to talk openly about it. He hadn't even told
his own wife he was reading the Bible! After much struggle with

his own shyness Luc prayed, "Lord, please help me to come out of my shell ... Guide me and I will follow You wherever You want me to go." Despite his prayer, Luc toyed with his own solution. Perhaps he could ease his turmoil by simply running away from medicine and becoming a farmer.

Instead, Luc took a one-year sabbatical from the hospital to travel with his family in a converted bus from Canada to the tip of South America. On a beautiful beach in Mexico called Baja Conception, Luc, his wife Lise and their three children found themselves camped next to Dick and Weezy Bundy, a retired American couple on holiday for the week. Luc listened as they spoke about a mission they helped and the doctor there who had to leave in May. Dick gave Luc a copy of *Charla's Children* and Luc stayed up all night reading until he finished it. God began to speak to Luc's heart. Before heading on to mainland Mexico, Luc and Lise requested an application from the mission.

Three months and many hundreds of miles of travel later, the Chaussés returned to Baja, searching for the mission where they had been accepted for a minimum one-year term. As the Chaussé camper rumbled and pitched over potholes, Luc fought the uneasiness in his stomach. He had been a loner in his faith and really didn't know much about it. Still, his relationship with God was something intense and personal, something he had not found in any "religion". What if this was just another institution, a group that claimed to speak for God but had nothing to offer but another set of rules?

Just two days later, Dr. Patrick Murphy left and the full weight of responsibility for the clinic fell on Dr. Luc. Each morning he faced long lines of patients suffering from the ravages of poverty – malnutrition, exposure and diseases that flourish where there is no sanitation. Weary mothers who had walked for miles carrying sick, glassy-eyed babies stared at him, silently waiting for hope. Men hunched by years of labor watched him, their dark, weather-worn faces lined with the frustration of the proud but helpless. Dr. Luc thanked God for the months he had already spent in Mexico learning Spanish.

As he served in the clinic, Dr. Luc began to finally understand what had happened to him eight years before when he accepted Christ, and why God had moved him from the beautiful, green Gaspé region of Quebec to the desolate, dusty hills of Baja.

Dr. Luc explains, "The Bible calls this being 'born again.' The Spirit of God transforms our being and directs us toward aspirations founded on the love of God."

But while Dr. Luc grew in faith, his wife struggled with her husband's enthusiasm. Like Luc, Lise had always believed in God but did not believe that God intervened directly in human lives. It took a miracle to change her mind.

One day someone from the outreach team brought Teresa, a little two-year-old girl suffering from severe malnutrition, back to the mission. They had found her near death, lying on the dirt floor of a shack in one of the camps. Luc recalls, "She was literally skin and bones and had the appearance of a six-month-old baby. Lise agreed to take her in. She tried her best to feed Teresa with a dropper but Teresa refused to drink. She was too weak. One day at noon, as we were coming back from the cafeteria with the little child in her stroller, we met Charla, the founder of the mission . . . She stopped to greet us and then, as a natural gesture, she put her hand on the child's head and prayed, 'Lord, heal this little girl.' She went on her way. As soon as we returned to the camper, Teresa started to drink milk from the bottle in gulps. It was the start of a healing. Lise was convinced from that day on that God is not so distant. He was present, eager to help us in our needs, and ready to respond to our requests. At that precise moment, Lise asked Jesus to come into her life."

One day Dr. Luc came to Charla and asked, "Charla, is it okay to pray for people with cancer?"

Charla notes, "Most Christians hear the word 'cancer' and their faith drains out from them like water from a sieve. Dr. Luc simply believed with a humble, childlike faith."

Taking Charla with him, Dr. Luc went back out to a shack he had just visited. As they stooped to enter the dark, makeshift hovel, they saw a skeleton-thin young man in his 30s lying on dirty blankets, dying from the final stages of cancer. Charla waited quietly while Dr. Luc tried to make him more comfortable and asked Jesus to heal him.

When Charla returned to the mission two months later, Dr. Luc rushed to meet her. "Charla, you've got to come with me!" He took her to meet the same man again, but this time he was well, working and already 30 pounds heavier! Prayer for every patient became the cornerstone of Dr. Luc's practice.

As time went by, Dr. Luc's fear of being drawn into a "religion" dissipated. He saw that the mission was operated, not by people committed to a particular person or church, but by people bound by a common faith in Jesus. They came from many places all over the United States, Canada and even Europe. They came from many denominations. They came alone or in groups, some for days, weeks, months or years. Whoever they were, they formed a united army committed to Christ, not only in name but in heart. Dr. Luc wrote later, "Each person was not living for self but for others ... This was a new world to discover."

As Dr. Luc discovered his "new world" of letting Christ live in him, he brought a new world of beauty and music to the children. Luc had studied piano since the age of six, taken guitar in high school and played flute and saxophone as an adult. One day, seeing how the children loved to sing, the idea came to him to teach them music.

It must have been a God-inspired idea, for shortly after, the mission received a gift of fifty recorders! The lessons began. Soon, the children were praying for other instruments. The mission had never received a donated instrument before this, but suddenly, instruments began to come in from all over – saxophones, trumpets, clarinets, trombones, baritones, guitars, concert flutes, and many others. Dr. Luc taught himself to play them all, and then taught the children.

Other missionaries volunteered time to teach and Dr. Luc took one day a week off from the clinic to nurture his budding musicians. After a few months, they formed a small band with wind instruments, giving two concerts a year. Children who were teased at school for living in an orphanage suddenly held their heads high. As the only musicians in the whole San Quintin Valley, they had accomplished something unique and wonderful! In December of 1994, Dr. Luc took his children's band on tour to Quebec, performing and sharing their testimonies in venues ranging from nursing homes to the prestigious Cathedral in Montreal.

Luc and Lise were learning to believe, pray and live as if God really **was** bigger than their own limitations. Early in 1996, Charla encouraged the couple to design a medical clinic. FFHM had no money or plans in the budget for a clinic but Charla instructed Luc and Lise to go ahead and design the medical clinic of their dreams, the one they would build if money were no obstacle.

They began to draw. A spacious waiting room where crowds of tired, sick people could sit comfortably while watching Christian videos. A play area for children. Real examining rooms with working equipment. A delivery room where even risky births could be handled safely. A maternity room for mothers and newborn babies. Clean beds for seriously ill patients who needed to stay overnight. An x-ray room, storage for medications and supplies, a laundry room for hospital gowns and linens – on and on they dreamed. Weeks later, they put their completed plans away, wondering if anything worthwhile had been accomplished by their wishful fantasy.

Almost immediately, an envelope arrived. It came from an anonymous donor who did not wish to be added to the mailing list. This was strictly a one-time gift. He gave specific instructions. "Use this to build a medical center." The check was for $100,000!

In June of 1996, the mission joyfully dedicated the new medical clinic but bid sad "adieus" to the beloved doctor and his family. In their five years at the mission, the Chaussés had ministered to thousands of God's needy children, fired by a fierce compassion from the Holy Spirit. But now, Luc and Lise felt God showing them the mission field of Quebec. They knew God had used their time in Baja to expand their faith, their boldness, and their love for the lost among their own people.

From the platform built for the dedication ceremony, Dr. Luc looked out at the gathering celebrants. Pointing to two men in the crowd, he turned to Chuck and Charla who stood next to him. "Do you see those two men? One of them will be the man who takes my place." Knowing by now that God would always provide for His work, Dr. Luc had just pointed, in faith, to Dr. Marco Angulo.

Dr. Marco Angulo

As a young man, Marco labeled himself a "seeker" – a name usually taken on by those who have not yet found a god to suit their fancy. Studying philosophy in Mexico City, he looked for God in the Eastern religions and eventually joined a commune near Ensenada where he met his future wife, Alma. Years later, the leaders of that commune, Benito and Rosa Maria, searched for Marco and Alma to share with them their new-found relationship with Jesus Christ.

"They talked about Jesus as if they really knew him as a real, live person, not just something they read," Marco recalls. "They had a peace and joy I had never seen in them before." The impact of their testimony, and Alma's own remarkable conversion one month later (see Chapter 2), all prepared Marco's heart for his "day of visitation."

It didn't happen in any church or at a crusade. Now a student in medical school, Marco was studying for a test on his grandmother's porch when, suddenly, he felt a powerful conviction of sin. At the same time, his surroundings took on a strange beauty and brightness – something he later understood to be the presence of a holy God. He began to cry, asking God's forgiveness. Marco explains, "I had always justified my actions, blaming my parents, society, anything. Conviction was a new sensation." Marco prayed, "God, if You really exist, change my life."

Although he was young with a promising future as a wealthy doctor, Marco already sensed the emptiness of his life. All he really wanted was his marriage and it was falling apart. He wanted freedom from his drug habits. He wanted to know more about this God who had met him on the back porch!

"I felt like a blind person seeing for the first time," Marco remembers. He headed for a small church he had seen along the road. An elderly man came up to him, prayed for him, and spoke to him under the anointing of the Holy Spirit. "Everything he said was meaningful at that moment," Marco recalls. "My conversion was not a step by step process, but an encounter in which God came to me."

Marco attended that small, Assembly of God church in Mexicali for the next six years. As God restored their marriage, Marco and Alma grew passionately in love with Jesus.

In 1994 the Angulos moved to the San Quintin valley. A friend invited them to visit the mission at Vicente Guerrero and Marco soon met Dr. Luc Chaussé. A year later, at the urging of Dr. Luc, Marco accepted a position as staff doctor at the mission clinic. Abandoning a successful career as a chief hospital administrator for the state of Baja California, Marco finally found his heart's desire. Ever since first becoming a Christian, Marco had wanted to be in full-time service for Jesus. God had given him a particular concern for the poverty-stricken, indigenous peoples that filled the migrant labor camps – the very people that filled the mission's clinic early each morning.

Dr. Marco didn't always wait for the sick to find a way to the clinic. Sometimes he went to the camps with people like Erma Fennel.

Erma was a tiny but feisty missionary from Calgary, Alberta. One day an Indian woman in town begged her to visit Las Choyas, a remote camp about two hours into the hills over rough roads. Naturally she agreed and prepared materials to teach a basic Bible lesson to the children and preach a simple gospel message.

It didn't take long for a curious crowd to gather and stare at this tiny, white woman with an ear-to-ear smile. Nor did it take long for the ranch owner to arrive, his truck roaring into the midst of the scattering, frightened crowd.

"You have no business here!" he shouted. "This is my property, these are my workers. Get off my land!"

Erma had no choice but to acquiesce and headed for her car. A hand tugged gently at her skirt and she turned around.

"Please, hermana, please come back." The woman's dark, deeply creased eyes teared with desperate longing. "No one else comes to teach us about these things. Will you come back?"

"I can't," Erma answered, immediately regretting the weakness of her words. What was she saying? Of course she would come back. "No, I mean, yes, I'll come back. But I can't come on this land."

The woman pointed to the road outside the fence. "We'll wait for you there."

One week later, Erma returned with Frank Tiknor, another mission staff member. Sure enough, a crowd of about 40 families stood patiently along the roadside. Erma and Frank got away with ministering like this for only a few weeks before the owner showed up again. This time, he laid claim to the road as well, ordering Erma and Frank to stay away altogether. Broken-hearted, they did not go back. Several months later, Erma ran into a worker from that camp.

"You have to come!" he insisted. "We are very sick."

Erma returned and found a camp devastated by skin infec-
tions. Many had high fevers. All the children had festering, open
sores that only worsened each day because of the unsanitary
conditions. She immediately told Dr. Marco, who agreed to go
back with an ambulance and plenty of medication. He brought
along Don Pierce, a male nurse/paramedic volunteer.

At the camp entrance, Dr. Marco spoke to the guard, explaining that they had come strictly to bring medical care. They set up
a small dispensary in the middle of the camp and stayed most of
the day, handing out medicine, soap and hygiene instructions.
Just as they were leaving, they passed a pick-up on its way in.
They thought nothing of it and pulled over just outside the camp
gate to speak with some of the people.

No one heard the truck turn around until it was almost on top
of them.

"I thought I told you to stay off this property!" The owner got
out and pushed his face close to Dr. Marco's. "You are a false
church and you are teaching these people lies!"

"I'm a doctor. These people needed treatment!"

"I know what they need and don't need. These people are
Catholic and they don't need you," he snarled.

"Look, we just came to see if we could help." Dr. Marco tried to
stay calm and find a way to break through the man's hostility.

"You are trespassing, amigo, and I will see you in jail if you
don't leave right now." The owner shifted his weight like a
fighter readying himself to throw a punch. His movement drew
Don's gaze to the gun tucked into his belt.

Don got in the ambulance and began to pray that God would
give Marco wisdom to deal with the angry man.

Dr. Marco continued, "If you are Catholic, then we have the
same God, the same Jesus Christ and the same Holy Spirit. I have
many Catholic friends and I love them."

The owner's countenance softened a little. Don continued to
pray. Suddenly, the man began to mention problems he was
having in his life. To Marco's utter amazement, the man asked,
"Would you pray for me?"

"Of course!" Marco exclaimed.

That next moment, Don and Marco realized they were witnessing a most supernatural scene. The hard, violent man who had
just been shouting threats fell to his knees, humble and weeping.

"Pray for me!" He sobbed before them, oblivious to his fine clothes in the dirt, oblivious to the shocked and staring crowd. Soon Marco was crying too!

It was a moment of divine intervention that possibly spared Don's and Dr. Marco's lives. Unfortunately, that owner's heart quickly turned back to stone. Frank Tiknor, who was also a Roman Catholic, visited him at his Ensenada home many times over the next couple of weeks. In spite of Frank's appeals, that owner never granted permission for the medical team to treat his workers. At their last meeting, Dr. Marco warned, "You will answer to God for your decision."

Harvest time came and went. Erma and the doctor visited other camps. One day, they recognized a familiar face.

"Brother, how is your family? How is everyone at your camp?" Erma was almost afraid to ask.

The young man smiled. "There is no one there. Gone ... empty." The fieldhand continued, his eyes looking up to the sky. "It was like a plague from God."

Erma gasped.

"No! Not the people, the zucchini and peppers!" He laughed when he saw Erma's relieved face. "Everywhere there was a good harvest, except at that man's ranch. After you left, his fields were infested with a blight. Just *his* fields, no one else's to the east, west, north or south. Just his 30,000 acres! Everything died. He burned his fields and left, broke and ruined. We went to other camps."

Dr. Marco Angulo and others have often remembered this extraordinary event as an act of God's judgment. "Love makes Him a righteous judge," Marco muses, "as well as a God of mercy."

Dr. Arnie Gorske, a retired navy doctor from San Diego, agrees with Marco. Dr. Arnie has donated time to the mission for a few days each month for several years. He has seen God's mercy poured out on the babies who are brought to the clinic almost weekly, dying of malnutrition and dehydration.

Dr. Arnie explains, "The hospital in Ensenada is big, much better equipped, but the babies don't survive. Here, they survive. I've always felt it was the prayer and the love. Because of God's grace upon this place, there is hope when there should be no hope."

One day, an urgent call came over Marco's radio (which stays tuned to the local police frequency).

"Fire in the camp!"

Dr. Angulo immediately radioed to the other staff members who have been trained as rescue workers by Chuck Pereau and Joe Vaine, the mission's resident bush pilot. Both are former firemen. Marco's son Saulo, a fifth-year medical student, joined the team.

By the time the men arrived, three shacks had burned beyond saving. Raging flames consumed the first home where the fire had started. Early that morning, before heading for the fields, the parents had left a small, two-burner, propane stove going in hopes of making the freezing, cardboard shelter just a bit warmer for their sleeping children. The cardboard ignited first, then the mattress where two children lay wrapped in the same blanket. The older one woke first, then ran from the home in panic. When the team arrived, Saulo heard the screams of neighbors.

"The baby is still inside! There's still another one inside!"

Saulo ran in, but it was too late. He emerged from the smoke and flames with a tiny, charred body sagging in his arms. The older child sustained major burns and was flown by the Shriner's Hospital to Sacramento, California for emergency treatment. He died on the way.

Each year, the mission responds to fifteen to twenty cases of fires in the migrant labor camps. Always, the root cause is poverty – small, crowded shelters of plastic and bone-dry sticks and cardboard, the lack of protection against severe cold, children left untended because every able-bodied person must work in order for the family to eat. They are poor, but they are not forgotten by God. God is touching young men like Saulo and filling them with His Spirit of mercy, preparing them to come and serve the people He loves.

After seven years with the mission, Dr. Marco Angulo is now serving with another Christian clinic in Tijuana. God is opening many new doors of ministry for both him and his wife, Alma. Before Marco left, however, God had already used him to connect the next link in the chain.

Dr. Ramon Avitia

The serious, soft-spoken medical student who wanted to be a priest listened to his intriguing classmate. Ramon hung on

Marco's every word. Here was a friend who shared his spiritual hunger, his fierce determination to discover what lay beyond the physical biology of life they studied in school. As first-year students, they dissected cadavers together – and contemplated the question of death together. Ramon came from a strict, sheltered home with strong religious traditions. Marco approached the spiritual world in a different way – he smoked pot. Together, they explored all things mystic, Eastern and Western.

One day, Marco gave Ramon a New Testament. Although neither one of them knew what it meant to be a Christian, they tried to understand what they were reading. Then, as mentioned earlier, Marco had his powerful encounter with the Holy Spirit. As Marco shared with his close friend, Ramon's own quest for truth took a sharp turn.

One night Marco began to tell Ramon he needed to repent of his sin; he needed to ask Jesus to come into his heart. As Ramon began to pray, it seemed as if the room was filled with an intense, bright light. He closed his eyes and dared not open them as an awareness of God's holy presence grew stronger. Later, he recalls, "When I read the Bible again, I suddenly realized that I was understanding what I read for the first time."

Instead of becoming a priest, Ramon began serving as an elder in a small church near the medical school. Quickly he realized God was calling him to something more than medical practice. Wherever he went, God brought people who needed spiritual as well as physical help.

Nine years later a call came from his old friend, Dr. Marco Angulo. "Ramon, there's a place here in the San Quintin valley where God is doing mighty things. You need to come!"

The invitation nagged at Ramon's heart. He knew God had never revoked his call to full-time service. As Ramon began to pray about this decision, he felt God working in his heart. When Charla offered him a job as head of the mission clinic, he was ready. He gave up his practice and joined the ranks of other $200-per-month servants in the dusty little town of Vicente Guerrero.

After almost four years at the mission, Dr. Ramon Avitia accepted the position of pastor at the mission's church. Still, he puts his medical training to good use. He teaches classes on health and first-aid for missionaries at the mission Bible school. Each Friday he flies with Joe Vaine, the mission pilot, into remote areas of the Baja to administer free medical care and the love of God to those who are hard to reach but not forgotten.

Ramon's wife, Ofelia, carries many responsibilities as she is both a pastor's wife and administrator of the mission's element- ary school.

Ramon is a gentle, humble man who comments, "It encour- ages me that God chooses the inadequate to use. That pushes me forward." As God continues to orchestrate the work of the mission, He sends others like Dr. Avitia to be a part of His master plan. Somehow God finds them – even if they're in Alaska . . .

Dr. David and Brigid Cammack

Dr. David Cammack came home from Fairbanks Memorial Hospital exhausted as usual. After turning on the T.V. for companion noise, he began to rummage in the kitchen for something that wouldn't take too much effort but might pass for a meal. The voice from the living room sounded familiar. Billy Graham. Must be a crusade on. David continued to scavenge, hearing the sound but not really listening to the message. Hadn't he heard it all before?

David had grown up in Bolivia, the son of missionaries. As a teenager, he sensed God's call on his life but that quickly faded when he went off to college and medical school. "I had a legalistic understanding of religion, but I had no relationship with God," David recalls, "so my faith was pretty unsatisfying. Little by little, I began to do my own thing and God wasn't a part of it." By now, God was distant memory, a phase of bygone youth.

David wandered back into the den. Something in the tone of Billy Graham's voice caught his attention and touched him in a way he could not explain. What was happening? Suddenly, he was weeping as a conviction of sin gripped his heart and drove him to his knees. It made no sense. He hadn't paid any attention to the preaching. Apparently, the Holy Spirit had an appointment with David that He was going to keep, whether

David was listening or not! "I'm sure that was the answer to the many prayers of my parents and grandparents," David now believes.

Meanwhile, out on the Alaska pipeline, God was touching the heart of an Irish Catholic woman from Cleveland, Ohio to be the other half of a powerful team. Brigid had accepted Christ at a Billy Graham crusade at thirteen, but with no one to disciple her, she quickly drifted into drugs and the hippie subculture. For many years, she lived in communes around the United States where she delved into organic farming, transcendental meditation, Eastern mysticism, and more drugs. Now a divorced, single mother, Brigid found herself on the wild and beautiful frontier of civilization, but bound by the ugliness of depression, alcohol and drugs.

"One day, my three-year-old son asked me who God was," Brigid recalls. "I didn't have a good answer, but I wanted one. Once, when I was around eight or nine, I had sat in a Roman Catholic church and prayed, 'I know You're there, God, but I can't find You." Brigid needed God to find *her*. During this time in Alaska, she feels, God was wooing her to Himself. She began to visit local churches, intrigued as she saw people worshiping a God they seemed to know and love.

One winter night in 1983, Brigid found her father passed out drunk in a snow drift and rushed him to the hospital. Dr. David Cammack attended her father.

It was David who eventually led Brigid to Jesus. Four months later, they married.

The couple grew in their faith together as they both sought a new life. As a child, David had witnessed the joyful zeal of his parents as they served the Lord with wholehearted commitment. He knew better than to settle for a lukewarm, half-hearted religion. He wanted more. Brigid had long tired of seeking happiness by feeding her own desires and was ready to try life God's way – seeking His will instead of her own.

A series of short-term missionary trips took the couple to every corner of the globe, including Russia and China. Then a group from their church planned a trip to Mexico, a trip led by Barry Wineroth of YWAM in Chico, California. The Cammacks had never heard of Vicente Guerrero, but every month, Barry took a different church group to serve for one week at a mission in this tiny town. When David and Brigid went, they took their twelve-year-old daughter Rachel with them.

It was Rachel who first began to talk about moving to Mexico for long-term service, telling her parents that she just "felt like that's what we're supposed to do." David and Brigid agreed to pray and soon knew God was indeed calling them to Mexico.

David shut down his practice, they sold their home and made the plunge into a lifestyle of day-to-day dependence upon God. "God has proved Himself more than faithful," Brigid smiles. "He is who He says He is."

"We've learned a lot here," Brigid continues. "It's not just the work that's important, but to bless everyone around you in the process. We come from so many different churches and backgrounds. We've learned that without unity, nothing gets done. We need to bless each other, not curse each other."

David adds, "In our churches back home, we hang out with people we like. If you don't like your church, you go to another one. In this situation, you have no choice who you live with. It's been good! You have to learn to forgive, to love, to not get all upset about stuff people say and do. We are all growing in the Lord. You learn to deal with disagreements in a Christian way – it's good exercise!"

The Cammacks have both served in the clinic for the past four years but Brigid considers intercessory prayer as her primary calling. "So many times," Brigid says, "we would be out of something and I'd be walking the halls praying for that need. Then, a day or two later, it would arrive."

David explains one of the important aspects of the mission clinic. "People can stay here who aren't sick enough to stay in the government hospital, but if they go home to their cold, dirty homes, they'll only get worse – especially the babies. Often the mothers are so poor, they have to go back to the fields and can't breastfeed. But they can't afford milk either, so they feed their babies rice water. Pretty soon, malnutrition sets in and the baby dies."

David has spent much of his time teaching basic nutrition and hygiene to his patients. Through the clinic and through the outreach teams, the mission distributes 300 quarts (about 1,200 bottles) of donated infant formula every month.

In April of 2002, the Cammacks left the mission to follow

God's leading to minister in Brigid's native Ireland. Who will come next? By the time this is read, God, in His wisdom and by His grace, will have already added His next link to the chain.

"The world and its desires pass away,
but the man who does the will of God lives for ever."
(1 John 2:17)

Chapter 11

The Volunteers: a River of Love

"Let us hold unswervingly to the hope we profess, for he who promised is faithful. And let us consider how we may spur one another on towards love and good deeds."
(Hebrews 10:23–24)

In Scripture, we're told to consider "how we may spur one another on to love and good deeds." Does *goading* count? If so, two women named Olive and Mary may have very unique crowns waiting for them in heaven.

In the 1980s, when large groups of volunteers first began to visit the mission, Olive and Larry Keeler brought 25 young adults from Camp Luther in British Columbia, Canada. Their first year, the group gleaned buckets of tomatoes from the surrounding fields. Olive, a former camp cook, taught the team to can. In the past, mission workers had been allowed to glean, but they only took what could be put to immediate use. Canning opened up the wonderful possibility of spaghetti sauce, soups and salsa all year round!

Mary Hughes, Jean Fish and a group from Osborne Neighborhood Church in North Hollywood visited the mission the following week. They heard about Olive's culinary feat and took it as a challenge. Surely they could put up more cans than that! So they did.

Each year, the friendly feud continued. When Olive's group traveled from Canada to Mexico, they stayed at host churches along the way. They always made an overnight stop at Osborne.

Mary, of course, used this opportunity to taunt her guests, assuring them that whatever they managed to can, her group would best them the following week. While Olive was at the mission, Mary would fax for Olive's daily totals, then pump up the Osborne team with the latest number to beat. Mary's group would always come the very week after Olive's group left – determined to win! Even the men joined in, working fast and furious, as the competition got serious. As a result of this hilarious rivalry for almost twenty years, these two women eventually "spurred one another on" to over 1,500 jars in one season! Everyone worked hard, had a lot of fun ... and the children were blessed!

The San Quintin Valley is now a place where three rivers converge. The first one flows underground. The second is the river of desperate humanity that flows from the mountains of Oaxaca to the Pacific in search of hope, or simply survival. Now a third river flows in from north of the border. It is the steady stream of volunteers that come to bless the people of Baja in the name of Jesus.

This river flows in answer to prayer. *"The harvest truly is great, but the laborers are few; therefore pray the Lord of the harvest to send out laborers into His harvest"* (Luke 10:2 NKJV). So often, individuals show up at just the right time, with just the right skills, or just the right gift. Each one is the answer to someone's prayer; each one is God's answer to the needs of the world He loves.

Angels unaware

In 1979, the administrator of an old convalescent hospital in Pomona, California telephoned. Did FFHM want their beds and all the stainless steel equipment from their kitchen? In exchange, FFHM would have to raze the building and clear the site. This would take intense, hard labor, but anyone who runs a faith-based, all-donation ministry loves the word **'free'**! Chuck, Dave Taylor, Bill Moffett and Nick Andruff accepted the challenge. (Nick and his wife, Zoya, were Canadians who spent twelve years working, scrounging, buying and transporting goods for the mission. They put 500,000 miles on their van hauling for Jesus!) This crew of four men made endless trips delivering equipment and parts down to the mission with just a pick-up truck.

Only after much toil and time had been invested did anyone seriously ponder the issue of *installation*. To everyone's dismay, nothing fit! At the time, the current dining hall was still under construction and roofless. Now it looked more like a junk yard, filled with sinks, counters, cabinets, exhaust pipes, and more. Specialized training is required to cut, weld and assemble stainless steel. No one had a clue how to transform the pile of stainless steel into the glistening, commercial kitchen designed by Mary Peterson, a member of FFHM's board who had taken college classes in Kitchen Design.

There it all sat, for the better part of two years! Charla finally said, "Chuck, we have to stop all this work salvaging and bringing down junk. It's just going to end up at the dump."

Chuck was not to be discouraged. "Charla, you've never purchased stainless steel kitchen equipment or you wouldn't say that. This is really expensive stuff!"

Charla retorted, "If we can't use it, it's junk!"

One day a Winnebago rolled up to the mission office. The driver said he was on vacation, on his way to Cabo San Lucas. He had seen the orphanage sign and turned off the highway out of curiosity. Could someone give him a tour of the facility?

As the tour took him through the unfinished kitchen, he asked, "What are you doing with all this?"

"Well," the hostess replied, a little embarrassed, "we've got a design but nothing fits."

The man introduced himself as Eugene Suta from Eugene, Oregon – a stainless steel sheet metal expert by trade! And, he just happened to have all his tools with him in the R.V. Eugene cancelled the rest of his vacation and didn't leave until all the cabinets, counters and sinks had been properly cut, welded and installed!

The mission was blessed by a similar "visitation" not too much later. Osborne Neighborhood Church took up a Thanksgiving offering to buy a pre-fabricated, commercial walk-in refrigerator/ freezer for the mission. So Anthony Arnold, the building over-seer at the time, ordered one out of a restaurant supply catalog. (This was the same refrigerator mentioned in Chapter 10 that Keith Durkin frantically called Charla about, asking for the instructions.) Once again, installation turned into a major issue. For days, frustrated staff members debated how to put the pieces together.

Wouldn't you know it? Another man tooling down the highway saw the mission sign and pulled off for a tour. Towards the end of the tour, the hostess asked him what he did for a living.

"I install commercial refrigerators."

Twenty-four hours later, the refrigerator was beautifully installed and peace was restored to the mission! The man left without anyone getting his name. Many thought he must have been an angel until seven years later when a man named Barney Coones came from British Columbia, Canada to visit the mission. Someone recognized him as the mystery man from the highway who installed the refrigerator. There is an "angel" out there named Barney!

The Master's builder

Chuck Mills, a second-generation brick and block mason, sat in the pew listening with spiritually-electrified ears to the guest evangelist. Although he had been a faithful church-goer all his life, somehow he had never heard this before! The words rang true and deep within his soul. God did not just want a tithe of his money; He wanted a tithe of his *time* and *all* of his life. Shortly after, when the pastor organized a team to build a church in Guatemala, Chuck signed on to go. By the time Charla met him in Oregon many years later, Chuck had overseen the building of seventeen churches in various foreign countries.

Charla was invited to be a speaker for the Gary Randall Show Supporters Banquet at the Portland Red Lion Inn. A friend pointed out the tall, stately man and his beautiful wife standing near the entrance. Charla wound her way through the lobby, keeping her eyes on target. Her bag contained plans for a 1,000-capacity church at the mission. After a brief introduction, Charla got to the point.

"Chuck, I have a wonderful plan for your life!"

Chuck's spiritual ears must have been open again, because soon he and his wife Phyllis, found themselves in a tiny trailer headed for Vicente Guerrero – where they stayed for several months out of each year for the next fifteen years!

Charla recalls how Chuck would wait for the busses bringing volunteers to the mission. As they unloaded, Chuck would watch for able-bodied men to recruit as building labor. Unfortunately (from Chuck's perspective) the busses seemed to be filled with 90% girls! Well, what God provides the mission uses. God is the sufficiency. Today a beautiful church, known as "the church that girls built," stands at the entrance to the mission.

No one will forget a day in 1990 during the construction of the church. Chuck sat perched high on an extension ladder, laying block without rope or scaffolding about twenty feet in the air. Suddenly, the ladder slipped and a startled cry rang out, followed by a sickening smack on the hardpacked clay ground. Chuck, an older man of 72, had fallen on his back! His body lay in awful stillness. How could he have survived that drop? Instantly, word spread and everyone began to pray – construction workers, secretaries and children. Chuck needed a miracle! To their great amazement, Chuck stood up a few minutes later and hobbled to his house. Later, a hospital x-ray confirmed he had cracked his pelvis but was otherwise uninjured. No one was more shocked than Charla who discovered him, six weeks later, on crutches plastering the walls!

Chuck's wife Phyllis spent many years in the mission kitchen that will always be remembered by many as the best years! This former camp cook worked wonders with whatever donations arrived each week on the truck. It takes divine gifting to make delicious meals out of dried peaches, Cheeto chips and tuna!

Under Phyllis' supervision, the sewing room altered or produced countless wedding gowns, drama costumes, school uniforms, draperies, etc. Add to that the mountain of endless mending that 200 children and staff can require, plus the altering and repair of truckloads of donated clothing. When Phyllis returned to Portland in 2003, the mission suffered a great loss.

But God is good! With His faithful eye on every piece of the great puzzle, God filled the gap with another talented seamstress, Charlotte McWhinney. Charlotte's husband, Ron, also serves at the mission. Ron is a self-supporting missionary maintenance man who takes great pride in keeping the mission in smooth, running order.

Youth with a vision

In the mid-1980s, a man named Barry Wineroth from the YWAM base in Chico, California began to bring groups of young people to the mission. It was Barry who introduced the staff to the King's Kids organization, which trains children in evangelistic outreach. At his instigation, and thanks to generous sponsors, nine children and two chaperones, Keith Durkin and Graciella Cordoba, traveled to Barcelona for the 1992 Olympic Games. They participated in the opening ceremonies, then stayed to minister on the streets through drama and music.

Because of Barry, and others like him, the mission receives over 2,500 visitors a year. What a difference this has made! Building projects that used to languish endlessly for lack of labor get finished! Volunteers handle much of the practical support work around the mission, allowing the medical, community outreach and child evangelism staff to focus on their ministries. Visitors go to the migrant camps, the dump, and the squatter settlements where, in spite of the language barrier, they are able to share God's love and compassion for the poor. Perhaps most importantly, visitors go home with a greater understanding of how God is calling each one to play his or her unique, vital part in the Master's Plan.

Praise Him with the stringed instrument

Nancy Benning says she heard God tell her what part to play nine years ago, as she was riding her bicycle. Nancy is an American who met her husband, Hans, while studying violin-making in Germany. They now own and operate a prestigious music store in Studio City, California. Nancy is an accomplished violinist herself. It is easy for her to understand how each person's role is important in God's "orchestra" of life.

"Go down and teach the children." She knew the Holy Spirit was speaking to her heart right then during her exercise ride. She and Hans had been visiting the mission since 1978, two or three times a year. Over the years, they had sponsored several children in the orphanage and developed lasting, loving bonds. Now God was calling her to a greater commitment and sacrifice.

Since that day, Nancy has faithfully driven over 700 miles to visit the mission each month. She brings instruments, music, and a lot of patience! Sometimes she persuades guest musicians to come with her and play for the children. Even the most poverty-stricken and illiterate, who have never been exposed to more than the passing blare of a car radio, are introduced to the beauty of great music.

Over 50 adults and children have learned to play the violin under Nancy's tutelage. Twice a year, her students give a wonderful recital for everyone at the mission, church and town.

In 1996, Hans Benning brought a team of eighteen Navajo from a reservation in Arizona. As the Navajo met with the Oaxacan Indians from Glen Almeraz's church, a miracle unfolded. Generations of inter-tribal hatred and prejudice melted away, replaced by a bond of love and unity in Jesus Christ. Hans remarks, "I've worked with the Navajo for fourteen years and never seen a man cry." Yet, tears of forgiveness and reconciliation flowed when these men prayed together. That group poured the cement foundation for a new drug rehabilitation center and has returned every year since to help Glen and Rosa with ministry among the local Oaxacans.

Hans and Nancy are representative of many who sponsor the mission's children. They give much more than their finances. They pour love and concern into the lives of children who have never had the love of a parent, or the security of a home.

Antonia is a girl who was brought to the mission at the age of five, nearly dead from malnutrition and tuberculosis. The Bennings sponsored her while Sam and Nell Greenberg, a couple on staff, nursed her back to health. Three years later, Antonia's mother appeared and took her daughter from the orphanage. Two years after that, Eva Shaffino, the outreach supervisor, recognized Antonia in one of the camps – once again sick and emaciated. This little girl was being abused by her mother's boyfriend and forced to work in the fields. The mission staff obtained the necessary government papers to rescue Antonia and bar her mother from removing her again.

Antonia remains close to Hans and Nancy, spending each Christmas in their home in California. She stays in touch through a steady stream of e-mails from FFHM's Tijuana house where she is living and studying for a career in computer technology.

Hijacked by God

Everyone makes plans. Mercifully, God often interrupts with a better one. Proverbs 16:9 puts it this way, *"In his heart a man plans his course, but the* LORD *determines his steps."* The mission has been blessed by many because God abruptly stopped them along the road, turned them around, and pointed them south. For example . . .

It was the late 1980s. A former Air Force officer and his wife pulled off Interstate 5 and drove through the guard gates at Camp Pendleton Marine Base in Oceanside, CA. Military families enjoy free access to the base campground along this beautiful stretch of nearly untouched coastline. Bill and Harriet Brabahm pulled their R.V. up to the hook-ups, anxious to sleep after their long drive from Vicente Guerrero. They had just spent two weeks at the FFHM mission where Bill, a master electrician, had volunteered his services to help with various electrical problems. They still had days to travel before reaching home in Beaverton, Oregon.

That night, as tired as they were, neither one could sleep. They thought about their trip and wondered, "What's wrong?" They decided to pray. By morning, they both knew the answer. Nothing was wrong except the last part – the going home part. In the night, God had spoken clearly to their hearts.

"Go back. You're needed."

The Brabahms pulled onto Interstate 5 – southbound! Back at the mission, Bill's amazing skills as an electrician did indeed fill a great need. New buildings, like the medical center, needed wiring. All the old buildings were rewired and the entire complex was connected to a new, auxiliary generator system – important in a land of frequent power failure. The Brabahms did finally make it back to Oregon – seven years later!

Jehovah Jirah, the ultimate building supply source

One day in 1995, as the medical center neared completion, Chuck Pereau went to "guy-heaven" – the building supply store – where he caved in to an irresistible deal. When he came home with $3,000 worth of ceramic tile flooring bought on impulse (at bargain price, of course), Charla was shocked and upset. Where did he expect to get $3,000? The next day, a check arrived from an unknown donor in the Mid-west written for $3,000 and designated for the medical clinic floor!

"Your Father knows what you need before you ask him," it says in Matthew's Gospel. He even knows what you need before *you* know you need it! For example, Charla readily admits that she never wanted an operating room at the medical clinic. She just didn't see the need when children could be taken to U.S. hospitals through Heal the Children or to Shriner's Hospital in Los Angeles. Over the years, Shriner's has provided hundreds of surgeries for children from the mission, particularly for burn victims rescued from the migrant camps.

In January of 2003, a letter arrived from Shriner's Hospital and the U.S. Immigration and Naturalization Service. From now on, children would not be allowed into the United States for surgery without passports. For undocumented, Oaxacan children in the camps, this was an impossible requirement. Now Charla understood why God had miraculously provided for an operating room. He knew the need and built it into the Master Plan!

In February 2003, Operation Blessing visited the mission for the second year and used the new operating room to treat over 2,000 patients. Many stood in long lines that wound through the mission property, waiting over 36 hours to see the doctors. Mission staff handed out food, water and blankets, trying to keep those in line as comfortable as possible.

After surgery on his cornea, one little four-year-old boy saw his mother for the first time! A young blind woman had a double cornea replacement and received her sight!

One of the awesome things about God is that He is not the least bit hindered by great distances or the remoteness of resources. He can see a need and find the answer – even if the two are thousands of miles apart!

Tomas, one of the mission's Bible school graduates, had returned to his home in Oaxaca to plant a church. About three years later, he returned to Baja. His visit coincided with Charla's regular monthly trip south.

"Sister Charla," he confided, "we have a church with walls but no roof." Tomas had traveled for many days and nights by bus to come and find help. Still, he asked shyly, knowing the enormity of his request. "It will cost about $3,000 to put a roof on."

Charla listened with amazement. The day before, just prior to leaving home for Baja, a check had arrived in the mail. Her bookkeeper and friend Lorraine Barter, had brought it to her attention.

"It's marked 'for church roof.' We don't have any such project going on." Lorraine asked, "Shall I return the check?"

It's a scenario that has repeated itself hundreds of times. Whether the need is for an electrician, a builder, a refrigerator, or a roof, we watch in wonder as God spans the impossible gap between great needs and surprising answers. What a thrill it is to watch a loving, sovereign God at work!

"The LORD *foils the plans of the nations;*
he thwarts the purposes of the peoples.
But the plans of the LORD *stand firm for ever,*
the purposes of his heart through all generations."
(Psalm 33:10–11)

Chapter 12

Oil and Vinegar

"Two are better than one,
  because they have a good return for their work: ...
Though one may be overpowered,
  two can defend themselves.
A cord of three strands is not quickly broken."
(Ecclesiastes 4:9, 12)

Children stared at them. Adults tried not to; most looked away after a fleeting moment of pity, their thoughts quickly returning to their own troubles. Mario tried to comfort his three daughters. The four of them made a strange sight as they struggled on and off the busses that carried them north, up the mainland of Mexico, and west, to the Baja peninsula. Mario, a tall, quiet, well-educated man from Hildago, near Mexico City, tried to stay focused on his quest.

Sandra, his eldest daughter, suffered from cerebral palsy. She had no control over her body, which made the rough, three-day-and-night journey even more challenging. Mario had to carry her, hold her up in her seat, feed her, clean her – all while traveling with two more young girls and all their earthly possessions. Staring out the dirty window, Mario reflected on what his life had become. A successful career as a school administrator, his marriage, his beautiful home, they were all gone, distilled into a beat-up suitcase and four one-way bus tickets to ... to where?

Once again, Mario pulled out the crumpled envelope and read the address printed across the top left corner – Colonia Vicente

Guerrero. A town so small, it rarely showed on a map. Hogar Para Ninos Necesitados – Home for Needy Children. The envelope had been sent to a friend five years ago. Did this place still exist? The friend didn't know, but Mario had taken the address and committed himself to finding it with the determination of the desperate. Was he a fool, headed for a mirage in the desert?

"God," he muttered. He spoke to no one really; he had no use for God anymore. "Please, let me find this place." Shoving the envelope back into his pocket, he took Sandra's flailing hand and held it firmly in his own.

There had been a time when Mario could say, "I have all I need and all I want." That was before. Before his wife lost her mind. Before she tried to overdose their children, then tried to suffocate their children. Before she burned down the house and destroyed everything they owned. Mario had paid for the best doctors, waiting patiently through two long years of treatments. Finally, he took the advice of doctors and family and divorced his wife of ten years.

The bus pulled out of the Tijuana station, turning south to wind down along the high, coastal cliffs. The beauty of the sun on the sparkling sea passed by unnoticed. Mario stared out at nothing, sightless with grief and worry. He could not pray, although he did remember praying as a child in some dim cathedral filled with the smoke of pungent incense and flickering candles. If God existed, he wanted nothing to do with Him. Right now, the idea of a God who could allow such pain only enraged him.

He looked down at little Lizette, six, and Mariana, seven. Exhaustion had crumpled their bodies together and their limp necks bent and bounced at painful angles. Mario winced, thankful for the flexibility of the young. He struggled against Sandra's dead weight and tried to shove his jacket under the two younger girls' heads. Nine more hours. Hours to figure out why he was here and what he was going to do when they got to, where was it, Vicente Guerrero?

Mario could not explain to anyone, not even his mother and sister back home, just what drove him. All he knew was that about a month ago, some inner voice began compelling him to go. He had no desire to leave his home town, his family and friends. And yet, there it was, an inner drive insisting that he go and find a place to begin again. He didn't really know what he was looking for, except that it had to be a safe place for his children, especially Sandra.

They arrived in Colonia Vicente Guerrero after dark. Carrying Sandra over his shoulder with one arm and dragging a suitcase with the other, Mario herded the two little ones off the bus. "This really is the middle of nowhere," he groaned, hailing the only taxi in sight. Mario showed the envelope to the driver.

"Of course, senor! I just dropped sister Graciella at the same place." The driver beamed, happy to please. Mario breathed easier. The place still existed, at least.

Max Christian, the director at the mission, greeted the newcomer. He assumed Mario had come to drop off the children and disappear like so many other fathers who came to their door.

"Follow me," he instructed. Max led Mario to his house where his wife, Alicia, made them a hot dinner – their first in three days. "You can sleep here. The girls can bed down on the couch and floor."

Early the next morning, Max left for a meeting in Southern California so Alicia led the family to a small trailer. "You can stay here for a couple of days. If you need anything, just let me know."

The trailer door shut with a click that seemed to snap Mario out of his month-long dream and back to reality. What had he been thinking? Why did he ever leave home? Here they were, stuck in a tiny, old trailer somewhere in the desert . . . strangers at the mercy of strangers.

Meanwhile, Max was in North Hollywood, discussing the new arrivals with the board.

"We don't have facilities or personnel to care for severely handicapped children," Charla noted. "There must be someplace in Mexico where this man can get help."

"I'm not aware of any facility that would keep the three sisters together," Max replied. "He's come a long way to find us, all because someone who used to work here told him about this place."

"That's amazing!" Charla wondered at a man who would come so far on so little. It seemed that God had somehow drawn him into a haven of safety and love. "Maybe the father and children are supposed to stay together. Do we have any staff positions open?"

Max hesitated. "Well, we do need a pig-keeper. That position only receives half an allotment, $50.00 a month plus room and board."

Max returned to Guerrero and observed Mario with his daughters for three more days before making the offer. Even then, he was embarrassed to suggest such a humble position to this obviously well-educated man.

Mario listened quietly. Slop thirty filthy pigs? His stomach knotted in revulsion. Then he thought about the few pesos left in his pocket. His last paycheck should be issued in about a month. He would wire his brother to send it immediately. Meanwhile, he had no choice but take the job.

Max invited Mario and his girls to begin eating in the dining hall with the rest of the mission community. To his horror, Mario discovered the orphanage was not only religious, it was Protestant! Years later, he recalls, "I was so bitter. If I had known this place had anything to do with God, I would never have come." After the meal, he spoke to his girls in the trailer, "As soon as my check arrives, we're getting out of this crazy place."

Mario coped by hiding behind a wall of self-sufficient pride. He worked hard and never asked for help. He attended the mandatory morning devotions for staff members, but tuned out the singing and messages. "God does not exist," he told himself over and over.

Christmas came. Mario dreaded facing his children. His check had still not arrived. There would be no gifts, no meal, no smiling relatives around the table. He felt farther from home than ever. A message came from Judith, the mission secretary.

"There's an envelope for you in the office."

"My paycheck!" Mario thought, racing across the central courtyard. Strangely, the envelope had no return address, no stamp, just his name scrawled across the front. Too excited to think, he raced back to the trailer.

"We have a letter," he shouted, holding up the unopened envelope. Lizette and Mariana crowded his arms as he tore through the paper. A Christmas card dropped to the table. Mario stared, trying to choke down his disappointment. He could not read the English words. He opened the card and found something else – seventy-eight dollars in American currency. Silently, Mario folded the bills, put them back into the card and returned to the office.

"What does this mean?" he demanded of Judith. "I didn't ask for this money."

Judith read the card. "This money is a gift to be used for a personal need. The people who sent it wish to remain anonymous."

Mario bristled. He had never received money as a gift and it stung his pride.

Judith continued gently, "God is blessing you, Mario. He has put it on someone's heart to help you. If you do not want to accept it, simply put the money back in the envelope and we will see that it gets returned. But I hope those who sent it do not get their feelings hurt."

Silence. Then, "Thank you," Mario whispered.

Shortly after that, another card came from a stranger in Oregon. It contained three twenty-dollar bills, one for each of the girls. When Christmas day arrived, the girls received more gifts than Mario had ever been able to give them. And more kept arriving! The women of First Assembly of God in Lancaster, California sent Christmas stockings, as they did every year, for each of the mission children. Mario would never forget the look on Mariana's face when she opened her stocking and found a beautiful doll with a porcelain head. Throughout that first Christmas day, many brought cakes and pies, tamales, candy and gifts to the family's trailer.

That same season, an old wheelchair turned up for Sandra but she couldn't sit in it. Her long, helpless body kept sliding out. With God's typical, perfect timing, Carol Knott of Courtenay, B.C., Canada arrived. Carol was a physical therapist trained in rebuilding wheelchairs for children! She and the outreach supervisor, Ramon Aguilar, worked one night until 3:00 a.m. taking the chair apart and rebuilding it to accommodate Sandra's body. When completed, a few days after Christmas, Sandra had mobility for the first time in her life!

Still, Mario had no intention of staying. In spite of the many blessings he had received, much stood in the way of believing what these people believed. Sandra had been born with cerebral palsy, his wife confined to a sanitarium, his house burned down with everything they owned. How could he believe that God loved him and had a wonderful plan for his life?

Six more months passed. Still, no check. One day Jon Cowpersmith came up from central Mexico for a special seminar. (This was before Jon came to teach in the Bible school.) He called the staff to a special day of prayer and fasting. Of course, Mario steered clear of everyone but finally decided, for some reason, to attend the evening meeting. Suddenly, Jon was asking him if he wanted Jesus. Mario squirmed. How could he say "no" with everyone watching? He agreed to repeat a prayer after Jon, but only out of politeness, then left.

"There's nothing in this," he concluded, walking back to his trailer. "I feel nothing."

Mario woke up the next day, surprised to find a new, buoyant joy in his heart. After "sala," the morning devotions meeting, Mario tried to slip away before anyone noticed his red eyes. He had never shed tears in public, but for some reason, he couldn't stop weeping. Almost immediately, he bumped into Corrine Ehrick, the office manager. They had never spoken before, but Corrine abruptly announced, "What happened to you today is the Holy Spirit. He touched your heart," then went on her way.

Later that morning, as a valiant sun fought through the coastal haze and warmed the steamy pig sty, Mario leaned against the side of the fodder shed. He felt strange. Was he getting sick? Suddenly, he began to weep uncontrollably. He couldn't explain the deep, wrenching emotions that poured from someplace deep inside him. He fell to his knees and remained on the floor of the shed for over two hours, overwhelmed by the Spirit of God and sensing a love he had never imagined possible. He began asking God to forgive him for things he had never confessed to anyone and vowed to serve God forever.

After that experience, Mario wrote his family, "I am no longer the person you knew. Mario Cordoba has died, and now he's another person."

Mario's paycheck never did arrive. He found out later that his brother had mailed it three times. Each time, it arrived at the post office in Camalu, a nearby town, where they held it for several weeks – without notifying him – waiting for him to claim it. He never did, and each time it was returned until his brother finally gave up.

Graciella

The little abandoned girl looked up at her housemother with wide, brown eyes. "Why are you here?"

Her question caught Graciella by surprise. Graciella found such joy in her job as a substitute mother, she never thought it might seem unusual to anyone else.

"Because I love you," she answered.

"I don't believe it," the girl replied, in a matter-of-fact, distant tone.

"Why do you say such a thing?" Graciella asked.

The girl answered without hesitation. "If my mom brought me here and left me, it's because she doesn't love me. If my own mother doesn't love me, then no one else can love me either, including you."

Graciella bent down, trying to hide the tears welling in her eyes, and wrapped her arms around the child. "It's not like that here," she explained. "God is the one who puts His love in our hearts, and His love never goes away."

"I don't understand," the girl replied. She gave Graciella a weak hug and looked again into her eyes. "But if you tell me it is so, then I will try to believe it."

Graciella had come to the mission as a single woman with her own profound understanding of God's love. Crippled by childhood polio, she still walked with a slight limp. At age six, in answer to prayer at a church service, God had touched her deformed foot. It straightened out and she never felt pain when walking again. Later, in a dream, God spoke to her that it was His will for the limp to remain. God used that "thorn in the flesh" to produce in Graciella a tender compassion for children who were "different" from others.

When not substituting as a houseparent, Graciella worked in the Child Evangelism Outreach Department – charged with reaching out to the Oaxacan migrant workers' children in the community.

"Ramon," she said to her outreach supervisor one day, "we need to pray and ask God to give us more children." At that time, about 70–80 attended their programs. Ramon heartily agreed and they prayed together, even though they could not imagine where God would even find more children in their small town.

Shortly after, around 1985, the migration of Oaxacan field workers to the Baja peninsula swelled to around 10,000 per year. Suddenly, the child evangelism program grew – past a thousand – to 1,500 children! The majority of children lived in squatters' hovels, makeshift shelters that sprang up on barren ground, shanty towns with no water or electricity. Sometimes they worked with their parents in the fields. The younger ones drifted like tumbleweeds, unattended, vulnerable, and always hungry. Coming from the isolation of remote mountains, they had been suddenly injected into a world of bewildering hostility, unintelligible sounds and painful prejudice. Because the smoke from cooking fires permeated their clothing and they had no water for laundry or bathing, they not only looked different, they smelled different. Graciella empathized with their sense of alienation.

"Okay, God," Graciella and Ramon prayed again, "You've answered our hearts' desire. Now what do we do with all these kids?"

"Disciple the children," God impressed upon their hearts. Soon Graciella was holding classes in various homes, teaching mothers and children. With other members of the team, she visited two camps a day, preaching, praying for the sick and helping with practical needs.

Graciella and Ramon began to take huge containers of milk to the camps to help nourish the children. At that same time, during prayer, God showed Charla a long line of children, each holding a cup or container of some sort. A man and woman from the staff were dipping into a vat of milk, but it just never ran out. A few months later, Graciella and other workers came back from an outreach full of excitement.

"Charla, the line of children today was the longest we've ever seen. They just kept coming. But every time we'd dip into the milk, it never seemed to go down. God multiplied our supply of milk! It just never ran out!"

In 1991, the newly arrived Dr. Luc Chaussé began to notice symptoms of severe protein deprivation among the children being treated at the mission clinic. At his suggestion, the outreach team began to hand out a scoop of peanut butter with every cup of milk. Once this distribution started, God began to provide in wonderful ways.

For example, Lisbon Bethlehem Church, far away in the bean

and corn fields of rural Newark, Illinois, heard about the peanut butter program. Ever since, they have faithfully sent their entire Sunday School offering each month for this purpose. On a recent visit, Charla was deeply moved by what she saw on the Sunday School wall – cut out pictures of peanut butter showing how many jars the children's precious offerings had purchased so far that year. Today, team members and visitors help to distribute over 1,000 pounds of peanut butter each month, one heaping spoonful at a time.

In 2001, Ella and Richard Westra, friends of the Pereaus and missionaries at the Oaxaca mission, were traveling through Quincy, Washington in their camper. Passing by a church on a Wednesday night, they decided to attend the service. Inside, an exuberant Hispanic worship leader was sharing his testimony. The son of migrant farm workers in Baja, Mexico, the boy had come to Christ because of a young woman who came to his camp each week, telling them of the love of Jesus. Vividly, he remembered how he would wait with the other children, grasping his little cup and anticipating the delicious scoop of peanut butter and drink of milk she would pass out at the end of her lesson. Needless to say, the Westras couldn't wait to pass on their discovery to Graciella who literally wept with joy that God had been faithful to grow those seeds she had so diligently planted.

Mario Y Graciella

As a single father with three girls, Mario was confused about more than just how to raise pigs. When issues came up that he didn't know how to handle, he would often turn to Graciella. Although he was a quiet, shy man, he felt comfortable around this sister with the warm personality and friendly smile. Ah, but what's a love story without a challenge, right? In this case, the challenge was Graciella's own complete lack of interest in getting married. Her devotion to her work in outreach left little time to think of romance. Furthermore, Mario had no desire to marry either. One day, the women's prayer group told Mario they had been praying for a wife for him.

"No," he protested in horror. "I don't want a wife!"

In spite of himself, however, the name "Graciella" kept pressing on his mind – so much so that he counseled with his pastor about it and sent Graciella a tentative note suggesting a courtship. Far from feeling flattered, Graciella reacted in shock and anger. Mario had always insisted he never wanted to re-marry. Now that safety net had been removed and Graciella felt pressured, rather than safe, in his presence. The next time the two met, Graciella vented her indignation.

"You're letter was very egotistical," she snapped. "I admit I've encouraged you to find a mother for your daughters, but there is nothing in the nature of our relationship that would ever imply that I should be that mother!"

With that, Graciella turned and stormed away. Mario stood staring after her in disbelief, as though hit by a whirlwind. Those who thought this was a match "made in heaven" were right, for, clearly, only God in heaven could put these two together.

Over the next month, Graciella calmed down and actually did try to give Mario a chance to explain his letter. Hopelessly embarrassed by now, and shy to boot, Mario never quite found the words to express the feelings he now had for her. Still, the incident started Graciella to thinking about marriage.

"Dear God," she cried out, almost in a panic, "I do want to get married someday, but not to Mario!" Graciella had always dreamed of marrying a pastor or a missionary, someone she could help to raise up churches. She could not see Mario pastoring a church. Her fears were calmed after a visit from Marta, another member of the staff.

"Graciella," Marta said, "God told me to pray for you because your future husband will be the next administrator of the mission."

What relief! Mario was just a pig-keeper.

Within weeks, Mario was called in to a meeting with John Moore, Max Christian and Benjamin, the supervisor of agriculture.

"I'm leaving now," Benjamin explained. "My time here is finished. You are going to be the next supervisor."

Mario protested in shock. "That's impossible! I don't know anything about orchards. I've worked most of my life in an office, not on a farm."

Max interrupted. "Things are different here than in the world, Mario. Here, what you know is not as important as what you are willing to do. Jesus promised that whoever is faithful over a little

– as you have been faithful over the pigs – will be faithful over much. If you don't know the answer to a problem, ask God for wisdom and He will give it to you."

Mario listened quietly as Max explained his new responsibilities – the experimental orchard, the two-acre mission garden, and the 3,000 young macadamia nut trees that would hopefully go into commercial production some day, helping to defray the costs of running the mission.

"We look for character, not ability," Max continued, "and for a teachable spirit."

Mario served faithfully, learning to rely on God. To everyone's amazement, he caught on to difficult procedures very quickly, whether it was repairing a water pump or performing a complicated tree graft. Soon he knew the names and characteristics of hundreds of varieties of fruit and nut trees from all around the world.

By the spring of 1992, Max had taken on the fledgling Bible school and Corrine Ehrick, now the mission administrator, felt strongly that her position would be better filled by a Mexican man. Once again, the board looked to Mario.

The news stunned Graciella. She ran to her room and began to cry, "No! No! It's not possible that he's going to be the next administrator!"

Without her knowledge, Mario's daughters had been praying that Graciella would marry their father. And Graciella, for all her stubborn resistance, had one overriding desire in life – to do the will of God. One night she finally prayed, "Lord, if you want me to marry this man, You will have to put love in my heart for him and his daughters, because my heart is closed." After that prayer, Graciella asked Mario not to speak to her anymore. "When God changes my heart and I am sure about this relationship, I will come and see you," she explained. That night Graciella slept well. Mario did not sleep at all.

The next morning, Graciella saw Mario walking very slowly past the mission laundry with his head down and his cap pulled nearly over his eyes, as if he was in hiding – or mourning. Graciella felt something jump within her spirit.

"Good morning, Mario!" she called cheerfully.

Looking back, Graciella recalls, "Suddenly my opinion of Mario changed. I saw his humility and it broke my heart. I knew he was the man God had made for me, but I was fighting. Now God has given me more love for him and the girls than I ever imagined."

Oil and vinegar don't mix – unless someone shakes them together and pours them out. Mario and Graciella were married on December 10, 1992 at the mission church! Mario became the mission administrator in January of 1993 and served in this capacity for the next seven years. Graciella became an indispensable helpmate, filling in wherever Mario needed her – at the T.J. house, at the center in Morelia, as a substitute housemother, wherever a hole needed to be plugged. On top of everything else, she created a place of beauty and rest in their home, a haven from the stress of running the mission.

It's still hard for either Mario or Graciella to talk about their marriage without a giggle at God's sense of humor. Who but a loving God could take someone's deepest dread and turn it into their greatest joy? And who but a sovereign God could fit such reluctant partners into one perfect whole, using each to support and strengthen the other in His good work?

In 1998, beginning with a vision given to Raul Garcia in the mission warehouse, God began to direct Mario and Graciella to Oaxaca . . .

Chapter 13

To Oaxaca – the New Frontier

*"So Joshua said to the Israelites: 'How long will you wait
before you begin to take possession of the land that the LORD,
the God of your fathers, has given you?'"*
(Joshua 18:3)

Raul came running from the warehouse, looking for Mario.

"Brother, this is going to sound strange, but I think God has given me a vision about Oaxaca!"

Mario knew better than to scoff. By now, his own life had been touched by God in so many undeniable and tangible ways. "Write it down, Raul. Write down what God is showing you and we'll pray about it and send it to the board."

At that time, the doors of Oaxaca seemed hopelessly closed. Lucio, the young man healed of blindness at the mission church, was FFHM's first Oaxacan Bible School graduate. Lucio went back to Oaxaca as a missionary in 1996 only to be martyred – stoned to death in the center of town by a drunken mob. Subsequent attempts to evangelize were also met with hostile and life-threatening opposition.

Once Alma Angulo came to Charla, deeply distressed by the conditions in Baja's migrant worker camps. She asked, "Why do you think God has allowed this?"

Charla answered, "I don't know. But maybe, since we can't go to Oaxaca, God is bringing Oaxaca to us."

Over the years, several graduates of the Bible school had returned to their native state of Oaxaca as missionaries to their own people. But rugged, primitive conditions kept them isolated and beyond any means of support or communication. They struggled with loneliness, tropical diseases and local persecution.

Raul's vision showed a base in Oaxaca – a place where pastors and leaders could meet two or three times a year for rest, encouragement and training. Raul, Mario and others began to pray about the needs of these dedicated servants and the possibilities of this unreached area bound by occultic tradition and demonism.

At that time Frank Tiknor, a chemical engineer from Wisconsin, was serving as host at the mission. Frank was a visionary with pioneer spirit. He affirmed Raul's vision and volunteered to accompany him to Oaxaca. Thus the Zapotec Indian and the silver-haired Swede were commissioned by the board to spy out the land.

To be suitable, the property would have to be centrally located, level for building, and have accessible electrical power and water; Oaxaca City would be ideal. The mission had no money for such a purchase, but trusted God's provision.

Affordable, level land is all but non-existent in Oaxaca. The people rarely sell their land; it remains in the family from generation to generation. After Frank and Raul spent eighteen months looking, the vision seemed more like a hopeless dream.

Finally word came that *five* parcels were available. Charla, Dr. Cano (president of the Mexican board) and Mario made the trip south to check out the options. Although one parcel was magnificent with a running stream, fruit trees and an ancient adobe hacienda, all felt drawn to a different 20-acre parcel with an unfinished building in the town of Tlacolula. The Covenant Church of Mexico owned this abandoned project which sat just off the Pan American Highway. Just as the delegation was going to meet with leaders of the Covenant Church, word came from the U.S. that a designated donation had come in for purchasing property in Oaxaca – $50,000. In the meeting, Covenant Church presented their asking price for the land – $50,000!

In January of 1999, Chuck Mills, the mission's master builder, went down to Oaxaca to survey the building and make plans for repairs and construction. A work group from Glad Tidings Church in Yuba City, California came and labored sixteen hours a day, hand-mixing and pouring over 50 yards of concrete.

Although the building was not completed, it was usable. Other construction teams continued to come from Valley Vineyard of Reseda, California.

During this time in Oaxaca, Frank Tiknor met an American missionary suffering from cancer. The man made a surprising offer. Would the mission please take over his orphanage with 48 kids? He was no longer able to sponsor or oversee the home. The proposed "gift" was in Etla, on the other side of Oaxaca City.

When the offer was presented to the board, there was more than a little confusion. Could this be God's leading? They had just purchased property and now they were being offered a gift of *free* land and the responsibility of 48 children. Charla balked. God had confirmed the selection of the property at Tlacolula. But Phyllis Mills, Chuck's wife, spoke with prophetic conviction, "We have to care for these children!"

"They need our help," Chuck added emphatically. The board decided to accept the property sight unseen and Charla and Corrine Ehrick were sent to Oaxaca.

When the two women arrived, they quickly saw why the man had been so eager to give the property away. The place was filthy. Raw sewage ran in a trench from the overflowing septic system and saturated the ground. Swarms of gnats and flies hovered just over the fetid surface. The plumbing needed to be replaced. Live, exposed wires looped across the ceiling, tempting electrocution. When the lights went out, rats and cockroaches scurried across the floors and up the walls. The children were ill clad and hungry. The propane tank servicing the stove had run dry days before and the children were gathering sticks to cook what little food remained on an open fire. At dinnertime, the children ate with their hands for lack of utensils. Plain pasta was served the first night, a piece of bread the second. Two young staff women were struggling to provide care in spite of the horrendous conditions.

Charla and Corrine just wanted out of this place! But after two days, their hearts resonated with Chuck and Phyllis Mills' declaration, "We have to care for these children!" An SOS was sent to Larry Swayze, a septic system contractor in Canby, Oregon. Larry and crew arrived a few days later.

Richard and Ella Westra, who were studying Spanish in Oaxaca City, volunteered to move their family to the orphanage.

Richard was a handy, jack-of-all-trades and Ella had run a restaurant – just the needed skills.

The Westras soon saw how God had used the two staff women in a wonderful way. In spite of the physical conditions and great hardships, they had taught the children the Scriptures, faith in God and the power of prayer. These children exuded gratitude and prayed for everything.

Now, with work going on in Tlacolula and Etla, the mission needed a permanent administrator to live in Oaxaca. Back in Baja, Mario recalls, "Everyone wanted to pray, but no one wanted to go." No one, that is, except Graciella. Secretly, she prayed for God to give Mario the desire to go and rejoiced when God answered that prayer.

In Tlacolula, the completed conference center now hosts pastors and leaders twice a year. In addition, the center provides a staging base for medical and evangelistic outreaches, sent out from the mission in Baja. Construction continues on staff housing, a Christian school and a new children's home that will house 90 children. Once completed, the children in Etla will be transferred to the new facility.

In 2002, the Holy Spirit moved upon the children of Etla in a powerful way. Of their own accord, they began to gather for intense prayer meetings that lasted for hours. Several children were gifted for healing. As they began laying hands on others, they saw God miraculously heal. When Mario and Graciella saw that God was doing something very special, they took the children out for meetings on the street. Children as young as ten and twelve preached with fervor, sharing their testimonies and the joy they had in Christ. Soon the children wanted to go to the mountains, to remote areas where the gospel had never been heard. Whenever their school schedules allowed, Mario loaded them into vans, fifteen at a time, and drove them for hours up tortuously winding, steep roads to the far, hidden peaks and valleys of the range. There they ministered through testimonies, music, drama and prayer for the sick. Recent outreaches have seen many, many come to Christ.

God is touching Oaxaca. In recent years, many Oaxacans have come to know Christ while working as migrant laborers in the San Quintin Valley of Baja. When these laborers come to Baja, they have an openness to the gospel which they cannot express in the hostile atmosphere of their home setting. As one Triqui man explained, "At home, you are not allowed to listen to Christians. If you try to go a different way, everyone in the village rejects you. You can't get food or water. Sometimes, they kill you."

It would be easy to look at the poverty and exploitation that plague the fields of Baja and wonder, "Why?" Praise God, He is the one who takes what the enemy intends for evil, and redeems it for good. What the enemy intends for death, He uses to bring forth new and eternal life.

Because of this clear move of God, the Bible school in Baja gives priority to the training of Oaxacan nationals who know God is calling them to return to their homeland. For the mission, Oaxaca presents an exciting new frontier of the Kingdom.

"I will give you every place where you set your foot, as I promised Moses . . . Have I not commanded you? Be strong and courageous. Do not be terrified; do not be discouraged, for the LORD your God will be with you wherever you go."
(Joshua 1:3, 9)

Chapter 14

Nut, Nuts and Moore Nuts

"The desert and the parched land will be glad;
the wilderness will rejoice and blossom.
Like the crocus, it will burst into bloom;
it will rejoice greatly and shout for joy."
(Isaiah 35:1, 2)

On tiptoe, John Moore might be able to peer over a five-foot sapling. But this elfin-sized man came to the mission with a giant-sized vision. A gifted agronomist who loved to experiment, John saw more in the dry, sandy desert than a water shortage. He saw the possibility of plants that had yet to be developed. He saw the challenge of adapting trees to thrive in a hostile environment. He saw the hope which a new cash crop would bring to a community struggling for survival.

Twenty-two years ago, John visited the mission in Baja with a work group organized by a friend, Inez Sorenson. Returning to his home in Santa Maria, California, some half-serious ideas began to percolate, then evaporated into the routine of his life. Two years later, John stood in his own backyard orchard, sinking his teeth into a sweet, juicy apricot.

"John, it's time for you to go."

John spun around to see his friend, Inez, standing under a tree with his wife, Ginnie. Instantly, John knew what she meant. The mission in Baja, visited so long ago, sprang to mind.

John began to make 1,600-mile, round-trip pilgrimages to the mission every two months. With permission from the board, he

157

turned one acre of weeds and rocks into an experimental orchard filled with over 650 different types of fruits and nuts. Dubbed the "Garden of Eden II" by the staff, John's budding paradise became the new home of cuttings and root stocks from around the world. John tracked down anything he read or heard about that seemed to have the traits he wanted. Ultimately, a successful plant would have to be extremely drought resistant, able to withstand high temperatures, survive sub-freezing desert nights, grow in the salty coastal soil and produce enough fruit to be commercially worthwhile. In John's vision, the mission could use this crop to generate income and, eventually, offer the plants to local growers.

With incredible dedication to his calling, John kept meticulous records of each experiment. He built a weather station to scientifically track data on rainfall, temperature, humidity and wind. As John wrote about some of his experiments and developments, agronomists visited from as far away as Australia and Israel. They came to see how he spread and trellised trees as they grew for ease of picking, the single tree with fourteen types of figs, the new avocado with a super shelf-life, creative irrigation – even how he used old pantyhose to filter sand in the pipes!

Some people thought of John as an eccentric dreamer but five years of persistence finally produced a winner. Macadamia nuts! No one was more surprised than John himself. Macadamias are tropical nuts that grow in moist, humid climates like Hawaii, not the desert! But walking one morning under the cascading boughs of fruit-laden trees, John and his teenage protégé, Brad Bertleson, knew they had cracked the case – or the nut!

The board agreed to let John use ten acres on the periphery of the mission but no funding. No one wanted to upset donors by taking money given for the children and spending it on an experimental project that might fail. John built a greenhouse but didn't have enough money to buy the mature root stock that would normally be used to start a commercial venture. (The macadamia variety he developed would be grafted onto this stock.) So John and Brad sprouted seedlings from their own nuts and soon thousands of styrofoam cups filled the 10' × 20' greenhouse, old trailers, storage sheds – anywhere they could find some space. When surviving sprouts grew to 18", they were transplanted to the field. Word went out in the newsletter.

Donors could help with this project by sending $15.00 to have a tree grafted and planted in honor of a loved one. Checks came from all over the continent and each new, baby tree had a name attached next to it on the irrigation pipe. Work groups helped with the planting and an orchard was born.

The second winter, disaster struck. The temperature dropped to 28°F for three nights in a row. Charla came to the mission and looked down the long rows of the orchard, her heart heavy with despair. The young macadamia trees looked dead! Two years of hard work, so much effort and money, gone overnight. What would she tell the dear people who had given to this project? How could she explain that their memorial to a loved one was no more than a dead stick and a huge mistake? She dreaded writing that letter!

A few days later, John arrived. Together they walked through what seemed more like a graveyard than an orchard. Charla fought tears of grief over the enormity of the failure. John's head hung low as he studied each frost-burned tree in grim silence. Suddenly, he leaped straight up into the air.

"Praise God!" John whooped. "We've done it!"

Stunned, Charla stared at John as if he'd just gone mad.

"Praise God!" John repeated and began to dance with delirious joy. Charla was bewildered.

"What on earth are you praising God for?" Charla asked. "This is a disaster! Thousands of hours have gone into this project and it's all gone."

"Look!" John reached down and snapped off a tiny branch. Sure enough, the center was moist and green. "We've developed the first frost-tolerant macadamia nut!" John ran from row to row, scrutinizing each plant. "Twenty percent survived. That's all we need! These survivors will be our root stock and give us another generation."

John rattled on gleefully in horticulture jargon. Charla understood just enough to know something wonderful had happened.

Over the years, Charla would recall that morning many times as a reminder of God's ways. So often, when things look hopeless from our perspective and a dream is dead, that's when God is working. He takes the very cause of disaster into His hands, and uses it to produce something new, strong and holy.

Over the next ten years, the macadamia orchard thrived and

was expanded to 2,800 trees, 1,500 planted as memorials. Brad Bertleson, the son of staff missionary Sonia Bertleson, flourished as well under John's jovial, enthusiastic mentoring. He later earned a degree in Agriculture from the University of Arizona and is now a leader with InterVarsity Fellowship Arizona. After Brad, John continued to train many nationals who still work in the agricultural field.

One morning in 1996, the phone rang in the Pereau's home office in North Hollywood. Dave Taylor, former chairman of the FFHM board, wanted to know if they were interested in a call he had just received. A wealthy businessman in Orange County was donating a property to the school district. Currently, the lot housed a large, 40' × 60' relatively new steel building. If FFHM wanted it, they could have it. **But**, they would have to disconnect the utilities, dismantle the building down to the last bolt, haul it away, and clean up the lot ... in one week.

Chuck and Charla knew how badly a building was needed at the mission to warehouse and process the nuts. The sorter, husker, dryer, roaster – they all needed to go somewhere – not to mention storage and a kitchen. In fact, they had already been looking in catalogs for just such a building. Charla didn't hesitate at this apparent answer to prayer. "We'll take it!"

Only later, as they stood before tons of towering steel, did they think twice about the decision. They had no equipment, no proper tools, no manpower and one truck. Chuck, retired now from the fire department, called Ralph Bigham and Vern Bachmann, friends who were ten years his senior. "Just great," thought Charla, "how are three old men going to take this building down?" She faxed the mission, desperately asking for reinforcements, but three days went by and no one showed up. Meanwhile Chuck, Ralph and Vern tackled the monstrous project with nothing more than garage tools, a rickety ladder and a lot of pluck.

Charla drove to the site one morning thinking, "At least I can help in some way." Her heart jumped into her throat as she saw Chuck swinging high overhead on a huge steel beam being lowered without a crane, just ropes.

Charla's friends, Gordon and Betty Kaiser, drove to the lot at noon. Charla had completely forgotten she was to attend a luncheon ceremony at the Hyatt Regency Hotel where the

"Selma Green Award for Integrity in Fundraising" would be presented. The Kaisers had come to pick her up.

"I can't leave!" Charla protested. "They need me!"

The Kaisers insisted, so Charla reluctantly left the job at the last possible moment and joined over 1,000 elegantly-dressed dignitaries of Southern California society in the banquet hall – still in her work clothes. It might not have been so embarrassing had she been able to stay quietly in her seat but, to her complete shock, she won the award!

Chuck drove all through the night that night to deliver the first load of steel beams to the mission in Baja, drove back, and continued to dismantle the next day. It took three sleepless, grueling trips that week to transport the entire building. At no time was it more apparent that God had truly given Chuck the gift of helps. Here was a man that doctors had said might never walk again after surgery that fused portions of his spine. He certainly would not be able to do any heavy labor! The incredible effort this job required would have surely killed him had he not been given supernatural strength.

After all that work, it would be impossible to express the overwhelming shock and despair Charla felt on her next trip down to the mission. There, out in the field by the water reclamation pool, sat a huge pile of steel beams, sheet metal, braces, bolts ... all hopelessly scrambled. She groaned, "We'll never put this back together!"

In the haste to salvage the building, no one had marked joining pieces or coded the parts for re-assembly. Of course, there was no manual. "Did Chuck risk his life for a worthless mountain of rusting scrap metal?" she wondered.

Fortunately, where the wisdom of man fails, the "foolishness" of God prevails. Why did God provide this enormous, steel jigsaw puzzle that no one knew how to assemble?

Three weeks later, Deanna Hoffman, a farmer's wife from Canada who came to volunteer at the mission, arrived dragging her husband behind her. Connard Hoffman had never visited before, but here he was now.

Connard took a long, slow look at the heap. "You know, I just put up a building like this on my farm."

Hallelujah! Charla could hardly believe what she was hearing. At the same time, Jerry Witt, a gifted mechanic from Bakersfield,

California, arrived at the mission. Connard stayed and three weeks later, under Connard's God-timed supervision and Jerry's skill, the mission had a nut house. Charla recalls this as a feat "beyond my wildest faith!"

But God had more in mind than just putting up a building. He was creating a new man. God used that visit to deeply touch Connard's heart. Today, the reluctant farmer and his wife are missionaries at FFHM's center in Oaxaca.

God often uses visitors in surprising ways – none so surprising as the time the visitors were bees! It was the spring of 1996. 2,400 macadamia trees, laden with fragrant blossoms, waited for pollination. John had ordered several hives of bees from Florida long in advance, in preparation for this exciting event. Success would produce the orchard's first sizable crop.

Then, devastating news reached John. The bees were dead, all of them, probably killed by insecticides used on the neighbors' flower fields. With only a seven-day window for pollination, John was frantic. He could come up with only one wild suggestion. Perhaps the trees could be pollinated by hand, using small paintbrushes. Pollinate 2,400 trees?! "No," he said, coming to his senses, "we need to pray." Everyone did.

Four days later, a swarm of bees arrived at the mission! Now, in all the years of the ministry, no one had ever seen a swarm of bees or known them to migrate through the Baja, but there they were, buzzing in a pepper tree. Soon, another swarm was spotted in a macadamia tree. Antonio Merino captured the colonies with ease. Then, a third swarm was sighted heading straight for the mission. They arrived and took up residence in one of the vacant hives left by the bees that died. These mysterious visitors were right on time and seemed to know right where to go! Fall came, and the orchard flourished in all its nutty glory. What an incredible answer to prayer!

The macadamia orchard is still a few years from full maturity, but the trees produce enough to supply the mission gift shop with a variety of nutty confections, from chili salsa roasted nuts to carmeled macrocha. Once they do reach maturity, the trees will bear nuts for another 75 years!

Why does a ministry to orphans and migrant field workers need a nut orchard? Perhaps God is fulfilling John Moore's original vision of a cash crop that will help support the mission and bless the local economy. Recently, one of the world's largest nut brokers approached the FFHM board with an offer to purchase everything the mission can produce for many years to come! Those negotiations are still in progress. Stay posted!

> *Instead of the thornbush will grow the pine tree,*
> *and instead of briers the myrtle will grow.*
> *This will be for the LORD's renown,*
> *for an everlasting sign,*
> *which will not be destroyed."*
> (Isaiah 55:13)

PART IV

Our All-Sufficient God

Early each morning, gyms across the land pulse with the accelerated heart rates of people determined to get in shape. Some force themselves onto treadmills, others pit themselves against weighted bars of iron. If God had a gym, what kind of equipment would we find there? Trials to build endurance? The burdens of others to carry for strength?

Physical goals are fine, but what about spiritual goals? Forget muscles, we need bigger faith! Can you think of the Holy Spirit as a personal trainer? How might He build our faith? What exercise is required? Walking. Not on a treadmill, not on an impact-free elliptical cycler, not on a stair-stepper. In God's gym, you have to walk . . . on water.

The mission in Mexico has always been about walking in faith. From the first decision to buy the land, few steps have been taken with any knowledge of how it's all going to stay afloat. There is only the Lord's command as spoken to Peter, "Come!"

But faith is not exercised by some abstract entity called a "ministry". It is exercised by people. It's people who respond in obedience to God's call on their lives and experience His all-sufficient power as a result. In Part IV, you will meet some of those who have heard His voice and climbed out of their boats, leaving behind the predictable and familiar in order to walk the waves.

Chapter 15

Life Begins at 40!

*"The thief comes only to steal and kill and destroy;
I have come that they may have **life**, and have it to the full."*
(John 10:10)

She stood trembling at the busy North Hollywood street corner, partially hunched over with both hands gripping her legs. Cars raced by on the green light, coming within two feet of the curb – a distance she could leap in just one second. "Jump!" The voice hissed in her ear and she pressed her eyes shut tight as if she could squeeze the tormentor from her mind. It took all her concentration to resist the suicidal impulse. Finally, her shaky hand reached for the light post and pressed the pedestrian button. Her heart racing, she leaned against the post until finally the sign flashed, "WALK".

Corrine Ehrick had once thought she led the perfect life. She was married to a loving, intelligent man, had five beautiful children and felt safely religious. She felt little pity for those with problems, attributing their woes to some personal failure or flaw. After all, hadn't she overcome a troubled, abusive childhood? There were no excuses.

She reached the church and once again, went dutifully through all the motions of the mass. Afterwards, she waited for a private moment with the priest.

"Father," she began, trying to calm the desperation she felt inside, "I come to mass everyday. I'm doing everything I'm supposed to do ... but there's no solution."

The truth was, things just kept getting worse. After twenty years, her marriage had ended in heart-breaking divorce. The man she loved had succumbed to alcoholism, lost his job and driven the family into debt. He lived on the streets now and she worked seven days a week in a losing battle to support her family alone. Her teenagers were slipping into drugs and delinquency; her fourteen-year-old daughter had not been seen in weeks. To top it all off, her doctor wanted her in for tests, suspecting a recurrence of cancer.

Her priest tried to offer what little hope he could, his voice compassionate but tinged with regret. Suddenly, an idea struck. "Why don't you go talk to Pat?" Corrine knew of Pat Durkin, a faithful pillar of the church. "Pat's had some kind of religious experience. Maybe she can help you."

Corrine's desperation mounted. One day she prayed, "Lord, either show me the answer this week, or I'm gone. I'm going to kill myself." That week, Pat Durkin called her.

At Pat's invitation, Corrine nervously arrived at a home meeting, wondering if she would have to do penance for attending. To her relief, she recognized others in the room as priests and nuns. It was 1969, at the beginning of a great charismatic outpouring of the Holy Spirit in the Roman Catholic church.

At the end, an invitation came for prayer. Corrine held on to her seat, thinking, "Not me! I don't even know these people!" Suddenly, an invisible hand nudged her forward and moments later, torrents of tears flowed as the Holy Spirit poured over her. Corrine recalls, "Even though I was very religious and prayed, I didn't know if God was really there. I had no relationship with Him. As these people prayed, I felt like my burdens were being lifted and placed on someone else's shoulders."

Corrine developed an insatiable appetite for reading the Bible and quickly realized she needed Jesus in her life. She met Charla and began to attend the Friday night prayer meetings in the Pereaus' home. One night she came home from church feeling like she would explode with what God was doing inside her. She laughs telling it now, "I kissed the walls, hugged branches, I felt so much love I could hardly bear it!" On a "honeymoon" with Jesus, Corrine shared her new-found joy with all 48 of her co-workers, going from person to person. Knowing her life, no one mocked her.

One friend asked, "Can you bottle this?"

Her family thought she had gone crazy. "I felt eighteen again. I danced, I sang all the time – so in love with the Lord."

The bubble eventually burst. Adding to her grueling work schedule, she enrolled in school two nights a week. Her missing daughter brought home a baby and left it in her care.

One night Corrine came home from work ready to drop in utter exhaustion. She shut her eyes, trying to get a moment's relief from the squabbling racket in the next room. Suddenly she saw herself on a beautiful, alpine mountaintop. A man robed in white beckoned for her to come. He emanated love that seemed to shine out from Him like flames. She ran toward Him and fell into His arms. As He held her, heat began to flow through her body. She could still hear her children through the open door, but she relaxed and fell asleep. In the morning, she woke up full of energy and joy. "After that," she says, "I went through periods of ups and downs, the trials never stopped, but Jesus was as real to me as any person I knew."

One of the "downs" included the failure of a second marriage to a professing Christian who squandered their assets and abruptly walked out on Corrine after seven years. When Corrine returned to North Hollywood, God used her old Friday night prayer group to bring comfort to her devastated heart. "I was frightened," she remembers, "I was 51 and starting all over again with nothing."

Plagued with hateful thoughts towards her ex-husband, Corrine felt like a failure, side-lined by God. "The Lord told me I must bless my ex-husband and forgive him," she explains, "but I didn't want to!" Eventually, she learned to pray a blessing each time she thought of him and her angry feelings were gradually replaced by compassion.

Through Charla, God began to call Corrine to the mission field. Corrine argued with God. It went something like this.

"Lord, I'm a lady who is all alone. I have no financial security."

God then reminded her she had once had money and lost it all. "Haven't you learned by now that I'm your security?"

"Lord, I'll go when I'm retired."

"Who says you'll live to retire?"

"Lord, I've never been to Bible school."

"I didn't ask you that. I asked if you would obey."

"Well, I'll go for one year." Corrine adds, "I was good at telling God what I would and wouldn't do."

Corrine packed for Baja, intending to fill the hostess position and work with visiting teams. But the departing hostess decided to stay and the director assigned Corrine to be the bi-lingual secretary and bookkeeper. Well, she knew *little* Spanish and nothing of bookkeeping, a job complicated by dealing with two currencies. She decided to try for three months and go home if she failed. "God gave me the scripture, *'I can do all things through Christ who strengthens me.'* I slept, cried, laughed and lived that scripture. In three months, I learned." By the end of the year, Corrine spoke fluent Spanish. Her mother, now an enthusiastic Christian herself, urged her to stay.

After four years, the Foundation board asked Corrine to take the director's position upon Max Christian's departure. She immediately said "no" since she believed the director should be a male, Mexican national. However, she agreed to pray, or rather, to argue about it.

"Lord, I'm getting too old."

"You're just getting started."

"Lord, I don't know how to be the director."

"But I do."

Corrine was indeed just getting started! She had just finished working in outreach for one year.

"Back then, conditions in the migrant camps were horrible. No housing, just cardboard. No water, no electricity. I remember seeing a girl of five taking care of a boy, three, and a baby, about eight months. There was slop right on the ground that I thought was the dog's food. Then the baby and boy began to eat it. I cried a lot when I first started. Then, I realized that wasn't the solution. I got angry and began to fight with the growers to get better conditions for the people, to build latrines, to teach hygiene."

Corrine recalls a visit to a boy named Andres.

"Andres was seven or eight. He lived behind the church and always came to services. Suddenly, he stopped coming so I went to find his home. It turned out to be a corrugated cardboard shack that reeked of alcohol. In the suffocating heat, two dead chickens added to the unbearable stench of the surrounding sewage and garbage. The despair I felt over the family's situation made a huge impact on me."

Corrine's righteous anger turned into a zeal to see God's love poured out upon these suffering people.

"One day a grower locked us out from coming to evangelize at one of his camps. We went looking for him and found him at another camp."

"You're that lady causing all the problems."

"I beg your pardon?"

"You're telling my people to revolt because I'm not giving them more money and better facilities."

"We don't do that. We tell them about Jesus."

"It's your church."

"No, our churches teach us to honor and show respect for those we work for," she explained.

That grower finally let Corrine into his camp and a good relationship was established. As the doors opened, Corrine met with other growers and bureaucrats at various functions. She spoke graciously of God's love yet never wavered in her calls for justice.

One day, Roberto Rojas, a wealthy rancher who had over 1,000 workers in his camp, came to the mission. He had come asking to borrow some tables for their daughter's fifteenth birthday – a milestone event that is celebrated in Mexico with great ceremony and festivities. Because he had never been to the mission, he felt quite uneasy. Corrine, who was now the director, welcomed him and explained that, although they had never met, she knew him by name and reputation.

As Roberto relaxed, he shared that he had been reading the Bible on his own lately and had many questions about it. Now Corrine realized why God had sent this man here looking for tables! The two talked for over an hour about the Lord. Later, Roberto told his wife, Lupita, of sensing a peace he had never felt before.

Later, when Corrine met Lupita, she invited her to a prayer meeting at her house. "I was a curious unbeliever," Lupita explains. "But I had no intention of going to her meeting."

Finally, Lupita did attend at Roberto's urging. After that, Roberto began to read the Bible to his wife. Soon they began to encounter passages that spoke strongly against idols and the worship of idols.

"This is just Protestant propaganda!" Lupita responded angrily. "You should read to me from a Catholic Bible."

Roberto went to Tijuana and bought a large, Catholic Bible. To Lupita's surprise and dismay, it included the same passages. Roberto began to carry this Bible to their church on Sunday. Out of embarrassment, Lupita threatened to never attend church again if he continued to bring it with him. By now, their children were asking many questions about God, the Bible and the church. In order to have answers for them, Roberto studied even more and began to read to the entire family for two hours each Sunday afternoon.

Eventually, the Rojases began to attend church at the mission and Lupita came faithfully to the prayer meeting in Corrine's home. Roberto attended the men's prayer meetings. One Wednesday night, an evangelist from Costa Rica spoke at the church. Lupita describes what happened.

"We felt, as we listened, that the Lord was breaking our hearts. At the end of the service we both went up front to receive Christ. The presence of the Lord we felt was inexpressibly real. I needed to be reconciled to God, to receive power to change my life. I thank God we didn't need an incurable disease or great financial need to motivate us to receive Christ. Everyone needs God. And the only thing that keeps us from seeing that is our sin. We love our sin too much. I also thank God that He was so patient with us. He waited until we could see that we were empty without Him."

An amazing transformation took place in the Rojases' lives. At the packing plant, Roberto stopped inviting his employees out to drink. Instead, he invited them to lunch and shared Christ with them. Roberto and Lupita asked Corrine about the workers in their camps, "What should we do to obey God?" Corrine told them to pray and ask God for direction themselves.

As Lupita had asked in prayer, God did indeed give them the power to change their lives – not only their lives, but the lives of many around them. Immediately, they started bringing food and blankets to their camp. Eventually, they had the cardboard and plastic shanties at their ranch torn down, replacing them with sturdy, block housing. Lupita met with other wives of ranchers and raised money to build homes for single mothers with many children, taking them out of the squalor of the dump and streets. When Corrine found an old blind man living alone in a filthy chicken coop with no shelter from the wind and rain,

Roberto built him a home where he was lovingly cared for until his death.

As the love of Jesus penetrated their hearts, the Rojases began to set an example of compassion for other ranchers. Dramatic improvements came to many camps in the San Quintin Valley – changes that years of political fighting and socialist campaigning had failed to produce.

"You think being a missionary is dull?" Corrine asks. "It's exciting! When I first went, I had a limited vision of God and then I discovered that He is so much bigger than that vision."

She remembers her years at the mission as a time when "I learned about serving the Lord – that He gives back more than we could ever give Him. I came to Him with my sin and my ugliness. He blotted it out and gave me purpose and beauty. I discovered a merciful God who covers me with His grace daily."

Today, after a four-year hiatus to care for her ailing mother, Corrine is back on staff at the San Clemente office. She travels about half of each year between the Baja, Morelia and Oaxaca missions, acting as communications liaison and counselor-at-large.

Looking back over her 70+ years, Corrine comments, "My life really began at 40 when I came to the Lord. I prayed, 'Lord, You're not getting much, You're not getting the best years – just the husks, but they're Yours.'"

Today, Corrine exudes energy and enthusiasm for her calling. "You see this old lady? Well, every time I'm on the mission field, I come alive – I feel 40 again! I say, 'Lord, I'll die with my boots on if that's what You want!'"

"The grace of our Lord was poured out on me abundantly, along with the faith and love that are in Christ Jesus."
(1 Timothy 1:14)

Chapter 16

Finishing the Race

"He has showed you, O man, what is good.
And what does the LORD require of you?
To act justly and to love mercy
and to walk humbly with your God."
(Micah 6:8)

The pretty, young secretary of the Philadelphia Church in Seattle, Washington smoothed her hair and checked her stockings for runs one more time. The crowd at the bus depot began to thin. Eleanor glanced around; the man behind the newspaper was too old. He couldn't be the one. She pulled out the crumpled telegram and read it again, even though she had it memorized. "Your package has arrived. If not fully satisfied, return postage guaranteed." After a year-and-a-half, Eleanor was finally going to meet the young, Canadian missionary pen-pal who had won her heart through his letters.

It was 1961. The war in Cuba had kept Jon from coming sooner. Every day Eleanor read of bombings, plane hijackings and fighting. Jon wrote that he knew his name was on a list of those to be arrested. It seemed she might never meet him. Then a call came from Florida, then the telegram from Montana. She thought her heart would burst as she flew to the depot, singing all the way.

Jon Cowpersmith stood in the corner, by the lockers, hidden just enough to sneak the first peek. Enjoying this bit of mischief, he watched her flit about the station looking for him. Through her letters, he already knew her heart, her dreams, her gentle spirit. Finally, he made eye contact and grinned. She was beautiful!

Six months later, Jon and Eleanor married. Because Eleanor was an American citizen, they could not return to Cuba but they knew God had called them to serve on the mission field. Jon spoke fluent Spanish and an opportunity opened for him to teach at a Bible school in Tijuana, Mexico.

They did what most aspiring missionaries do; they sought pledges of support to ensure their livelihood while on the field. Next to nothing materialized. Yet, Eleanor recalls, "It never occurred to us to *not* go." For Jon, trusting God to provide had already become his normal way of life. The prospect was more difficult for Eleanor to accept. "I was a working girl, used to regular paychecks. I thought living by faith was going to be really hard. But I found it wasn't. I've lived day by day for many years now, with God providing miraculously in many, many ways." Jon and Eleanor never made another personal appeal for support. Eleanor adds, "It's easy when you know you are where God wants you."

For the next seven years, the Cowpersmiths lived in a trailer park at the Mexican border. Jon crossed the border daily to teach in Tijuana. Eleanor kept busy raising their two sons and working with children in her neighborhood. Once a week, they visited inmates of the Tijuana jail. One of those former inmates is now a pastor.

In the late '70s, Jon felt God prompting him to accept a call to Guanajuato, deep in the heart of Mexico.

"Are you sure?" Eleanor asked Jon. She still held her mother's letter in her hand. It said much the same thing as all the other letters from friends and relatives. Don't go. It was a year of great instability in Mexico. The peso had dropped drastically and talk of revolution was in the air. Other missionaries were leaving the country, not going in. Be practical, the letters advised.

Eleanor knew the practical obstacles. They had no reliable support, their children would be taken out of a good school, they needed the money from their house-trailer and it was proving impossible to sell. The letter reminded her of all the reasons to stay.

Jon smiled. "Who do you want me to listen to?"

Eleanor sighed. If she was learning anything, it was this; her husband took his orders from God and she needed to trust that leadership.

They left much behind, but there was one thing Eleanor could not bear to part with – her antique china cabinet. So they loaded their old car and a small trailer, tied the cabinet on top and headed south. At the Texas/Mexico border, an agent asked where they were headed. When they told him, he burst out, "They'll tan you alive down there!"

It was a bit like when the Israelites were told to cross the Jordan river into Canaan. The flooded river seemed a dangerous and insurmountable obstacle. Yet, the moment they obeyed and stepped in, God stopped the waters and they crossed in perfect safety. Eleanor explains, "Everything was against us, but as soon as we crossed the border, everything went for us."

One by one, the problems evaporated. The trailer they had left behind sold, and Jon was able to return for the money. Their boys, now thirteen and fourteen, immediately experienced a touch from the Holy Spirit that changed their lives forever. Eleanor explains, "At home, they were so bored in church. They just sat there; they never sang or participated. But as soon as we got to the little church in Guanajuato, they were filled with the Holy Spirit and got really turned on for the Lord."

Jon and Eleanor worked among local people who, for the most part, lived in camps on government-owned "ranchos" – contracted farmland. Every night of the week, Jon visited them in their cramped hovels, teaching the Bible and praying for the sick.

Jon's desire for a Bible school turned into a training-on-the-go program. His students worked long days in the fields or in the nearby oil refinery, so classroom time was impractical. Instead, Jon took his students with him as he visited his scattered congregation.

Eleanor found women to join her in visits to homes and hospitals. "One day," she tells, "we came to the hospital to visit a dying man. His wife was there with his grave clothes. We prayed for him and God healed him. Another time, a dying woman's daughters were sitting outside crying. We felt so bad for them. We asked if we could pray for their mother; she was in a coma. God raised her up right then. My ladies had such faith!"

The Cowpersmiths found the people of Guanajuato to be highly superstitious and hostile at first, to the gospel message. But by the time they left fourteen years later, many churches had been planted throughout the region.

In 1989 FFHM's mission in Baja desperately needed a well-qualified teacher for their fledgling Bible school. Once again, the china cabinet was tied to the top of an old wagon as the Cowpersmiths moved west to the peninsula.

For the next eleven years, Jon devoted himself to his eager students at the Bible school in Vicente Guerrero. Eleanor quickly committed herself to the inmates of local prisons in the San Quintin Valley. For five years, she directed the prison outreach, becoming a surrogate mother who brought love, comfort and the peace of God to many troubled hearts.

Even after reaching his 70s, Jon refused to ask anything of his students that he was not willing to do himself. When a team of Bible school students went to the rugged mountains of Oaxaca for an evangelistic outreach, Jon and Eleanor went too. For six weeks, these veteran warriors for Jesus slept on hard ground, went without baths or recognizable food, and hiked steep trails to reach the remotest hamlets. When a friend asked Jon what he and Eleanor did on that trip, he replied, "We washed dishes. And then we washed more dishes!" It turned out that there simply weren't enough dishes to go around so they had to be constantly cycled in order for everyone to eat. Jon, a master teacher, didn't just talk about servanthood and humility with words in a classroom, he taught with his life.

Jon died in October of 2001, at the age of 75. Upon news of his death, a former Oaxacan student wrote, "Woe to me if I don't make an effort to run that race, to teach others what my professor taught me ... Woe to me if I don't proclaim the Good News and bear good fruit ... as a pilgrim in this world. I will not forget the love and the teaching of my teacher." That student, Severiano Flores Ramirez, is now a church planter among the Triqui people in Copala, Oaxaca.

Jon brought honor to Christ even as his own life was ebbing away at Saddleback Memorial Hospital in Laguna Hills, California. His two nurses, Laurie Carson and Judy Krieg, were deeply impacted as they witnessed a man leaving this world with great joy and peace. When Jon requested to die in his beloved Mexico, they insisted on coming along to care for him to the end at no charge. Laurie has since made several trips to Vicente Guerrero and Oaxaca and knows God is calling her to full-time missionary service.

Eleanor looks back over more than 40 years as a missionary. Would she recommend this life? "Oh yes!" she exclaims. Her sweet, grandmotherly face blooms into a big smile as she pours tea from an exquisite piece of fine china. (Yes, she still has the cabinet!) She has created an oasis of beauty and hospitality in the midst of the harsh realities that surround her. After cutting her guest a piece from one of her famous pies, she continues, "It's sure not a boring life. Seeing God provide, seeing Him work – it's exciting."

She admits that as a child, growing up in a Christian family, she had always dreamed of serving God. "I never felt capable, but I had the desire." She laughs, "I wasn't very smart or talented. Whenever there was something to be done at church, they asked someone else. And look what happened. I'm a very ordinary person but God has given me an extraordinary life!"

"I have fought the good fight, I have finished the race,
I have kept the faith. Now there is in store for me the crown
of righteousness, which the Lord, the righteous Judge,
will award to me on that day – and not only to me,
but also to all who have longed for his appearing."
(2 Timothy 4:7–8)

Chapter 17

Isn't He Good?

*"Surely goodness and mercy shall follow me
all the days of my life;
and I will dwell in the house of the L*ORD
for ever."
(Psalm 23:6)

The phone rang. It was Mauricio – again. Eva clenched the receiver, trying to keep her fiery temper in check. Her family came from Mexico but some ancestral, Italian blood still ran hot in her short, feisty frame.

"Mama, please, this is important. Jesus loves you."

"You're calling me collect from Cleveland just to tell me that?" Eva slammed the phone down for the second time.

She lived alone in Torrance, California. Her eldest son Alex lived nearby, but Alex was busy. Suddenly, her apartment felt very empty. Maybe she should have stayed in Cleveland where she could keep an eye on that silly boy of hers.

The sharp jangle of the phone startled her. She snatched at the receiver and almost shouted. "Stop wasting my money!" Still, before the click could sever his voice, she heard it again.

"Mama, listen. Jesus loves you!"

Eva snorted at the walls. He called for that? Stupid son. She stared at the phone. Silent. Good, he's given up. Maybe Jesus will tell him to get a job.

The silence seemed to grow. She thought about the few words Mauricio had been able to blurt out. Eva began to wonder.

179

"What if it's true, eh? Just what if it is? No one else loves me. Wouldn't it be great if it is true?"

Eva looked at her watch. The dentist! She had to hurry. Weaving through traffic, Eva thought again about her son's message. So simple, so naive. True? Bah! Well, maybe she should give God a chance. So far, the odds were stacked against Him. Where was God when her husband walked out on her for a younger woman years ago? Didn't her friends say she looked like that famous movie star, Ann Bancroft, back then? Her heart and pride still smarted from that one.

Eva's face brightened as a plan formed in her skeptical, yet wishful mind. "Hah, that's it!" She turned to look up at the smoggy, metro-L.A. sky. "God, if You're real, let me feel no pain at the dentist today."

"Aaaaggh!" Eva's knuckles went white as her nails dug into the green vinyl upholstery of the dental chair. So much for Jesus loving her. She spit into the bowl, disappointed and angry.

On the way home, Eva turned west. A walk on the beach would do her good. Her mouth throbbed as the anesthesia began to wear off. She was certainly going to tell Mauricio about this! What a fool he was. What a fool he had made out of her!

Standing on the beach, Eva gazed out to the horizon. Something happened then that she would never really be able to explain. Was it the setting sun flaming across the ignited sea? Was it just something sensed and seen in her spirit? She called it a "ball of light" that moved towards her from the ocean. As it enveloped her, an overwhelming feeling of love and joy filled her heart.

Back home, still trembling with awe, Eva picked up the phone. "Mauricio?"

"Mama, what's happened?"

"I'm not sure, but you're right. Jesus does love me. What do I do now?"

Eva's son, Mauricio, soon moved out to join his mother in California where they attended church together for the next year. During that time Eva met Olive Thayer, Charla's mother, at church. Through Olive, Eva began to hear stories about an orphanage in Mexico. Although Eva was working as a teacher's aide, she felt a growing dissatisfaction with her life. She explains,

"I felt like I was living like an animal. Eat, work, sleep ... eat, work, sleep. My life had no real meaning." The thought of serving God by serving others on the mission field stirred her heart. Three months after applying to the mission, she was accepted as a volunteer for one month.

"My first day, I peeled potatoes. Then I squeezed oranges. My second day, I watched kids in one of the houses. It didn't seem like much, but I was happy!"

Still a young Christian, Eva was learning to seek after God's plan for her life. She quickly learned that that plan required faith. Everything she owned was now condensed down to one storage unit back in California. Not much, but still it did require a $50-per-month rental fee. She asked the mission director if she could be paid just $50 a month.

"No," he replied. "There are no more funds available for staff. Your position is strictly a volunteer one."

Certain that God had brought her to Vicente Guerrero, Eva began to look for a job anywhere in the San Quintin valley – a job that would provide her storage fee and allow her to continue serving at the mission. Just as every door seemed to be closing, Nick and Zoya Andruff, directors of outreach, came to Eva. (The outreach ministry had its own budget back then.) They offered Eva a job for exactly $50 a month.

For the next two years, Eva served in outreach, eventually taking over for Nick and Zoya. Her adventures in faith had just begun. Today, having spent the bulk of the past sixteen years at the mission, Eva recalls some of her more memorable lessons in trust.

"During a visit to my son in California, I attended a church service. Through a prophecy, God assured me with the words, 'I am going to take care of you.' That meant a lot to me because I was getting older and had nothing to my name. I was living at the mission in a trailer so small we called it 'the egg.' You could touch everything in the trailer from one spot."

Shortly after, a larger trailer arrived at the mission marked, "for Eva." Someone had donated the trailer to Olive, Charla's mother, and Olive remembered her friend's need.

"Isn't God wonderful?" Eva exclaims. "He just loves to bless us!" She is bursting with another story, another testament to God's goodness in her life.

"When I applied for Social Security, I told the truth, that I live in Mexico. Well, if your address isn't in the United States, they won't send your check. It wasn't very much, but still I needed it for things like gas in my car. I can get most of what I need from donations to the mission, like shoes when they have my size but," Eva breaks into gales of laughter, "you can't wear second-hand underwear! I needed *some* money!"

"Well," Eva continues with a sparkle in her eyes, "I had also been wanting to build a small house but, of course, I had no money for that. I was asking God, 'Why? Why aren't You allowing me to receive my Social Security check after all my years of working?' Finally, after one year, they released my money and a check arrived for all the back payments. It was exactly the amount I needed to buy the lot for my house!" Eva hoots with glee. "You see? My heavenly Father knows me so well. He knows I would *never* have saved the money myself. If I have money, I spend it."

Eva proudly gives a tour of her cozy, little one-bedroom house just a half-mile off the mission's property. She waves at the pavers on the floor and points to the tiled roof. "Whenever I needed money to pay workers or buy materials, I would go to my bank and the money was there." She shrugs in bewilderment and then grins. "I don't know where the money came from except that God put it there! Isn't He good?"

At 75, Eva still serves with her unique blend of energy, mischief and joy. Technically retired, she continues to operate the mission's bookstore and spends each free evening personally discipling or witnessing to someone in her neighborhood.

Among her many vivid memories, she recalls one special day from the time she spent in outreach . . .

The outreach van labored through rocky fields, fighting the slope of the hills and the battering of an icy wind off the ocean three miles to the west. Clusters of migrant families began to appear from their hovels. Children pointed and called out to others. By the time the van reached the main yard of the camp, hundreds stood huddling, waiting in the gray shadows of the low, damp fog.

Eva climbed out, knowing every eye was on her as she pulled open the back door of the van. Blankets! The team had promised to come back with blankets and here they were. Nick and Zoya had carefully counted, recounted and packed 600 blankets bought in Ensenada with designated funds. Children in threadbare, torn T-shirts jostled for position, squirming with the tension of trained politeness versus desperate need. Eva tried not to show how cold she was. If they could handle it, so could she. After all, she had a sweater!

Mechanically, she began to hand out the neatly folded, multi-colored Mexican blankets. Grabbing one from the box, another hand would snatch it from hers. "Gracias! Dios te bendiga!" Turn. Grab another one. "Gracias! God bless you!" Again. Again. Box after box was emptied. Eva paused just long enough to look up at the line of people and gasped. There were still so many! The line stretched and disappeared into the fog. Only one box of blankets remained. She could hardly bear to look into the hopeful faces that still pressed around the van. "God," she cried out silently, "please solve this problem!" Turn. Grab another blanket. Another frantic, grateful hand stretched out and the blanket disappeared. Turn. Reach into the box again.

Had another hour passed? Eva wasn't sure. The very last person in line walked away, a blanket under her arm. That nearly-empty box had not run out – until now. The realization of what had just happened hit her. It was beyond words. She could only sit on the dusty bumper of the empty van and cry.

Eva will never forget the phone call that started her relationship with God.

"Jesus loves you, Mama."

So simple.

Those words that once seemed foolish and naive have now stood the test of time and troubles. Eva seems to always have another story to share. Inevitably, her story ends with a finger wagging towards heaven as she shakes her head and laughs with unbridled glee, "Isn't God good?"

> *"The LORD is good,*
> *a refuge in times of trouble.*
> *He cares for those who trust in him ... "*
> (Nahum 1:7)

Chapter 18

Treasure Found

"What good is it for a man to gain the whole world,
yet forfeit his soul?"
(Mark 8:36)

It's 7:00 a.m. and a rising sun flames over the cactus-pinned hills of the Baja desert, backlighting their profile into dark shoulders that hunch against a bright, cloudless sky. The night's chill quickly dissipates under the solar onslaught. A faded orange windsock hangs limp in the still, morning air. Joe Vaine, pilot of a six-passenger Cessna 206, opens the hangar door. His passengers peel off sweatshirts and don sunglasses.

Today Joe, Dr. Ramon Avitia and Alma Vargas, a nurse from the mission clinic, will fly a medical outreach to Santa Rosalillita, a small fishing village 200 miles to the south. The plane is loaded with four black duffel bags of medical equipment and supplies.

Joe cleans the desert dust off all the windows and wipes over the broad, red letters that dance across the plane's nose, "Flying for Jesus." Dr. Avitia has flown these Friday outreaches with Joe for many years and knows better than to offer his help. Joe is what every passenger likes to see in a pilot. He is methodical and deliberate, entirely focused on his routine. Alma waits through the safety check in subdued silence. Finally she admits with a nervous laugh, "I don't like to fly!" Soon, everyone is pushing the plane out onto the rutted, pebble-strewn airstrip. Joe hands out headsets – necessary to mute the engine's deafening roar and facilitate conversation through the built-in microphones.

"Clear prop!" Joe barks out the window, then ignites the

engine. There is no one around except two young boys on one bike, raising a billow of dust at the edge of the field. Still, safety rules do not get bent. The Cessna bounces to life and trembles on her wheels, as if in anticipation.

Soon the small party is droning over an expanse so vast and empty that the plane seems no bigger than a mosquito. The small size is an advantage, Joe explains. She can take-off and land on short or soft strips that a larger, heavier plane would find impossible.

An hour and fifteen minutes later, "Flying for Jesus" circles over a bluff-top strip that is both short and soft – and now everyone understands why Joe loves this little plane. The runway is an illegal strip that soldiers usually have covered with boulders to prevent its use, presumably by drug dealers. A few years ago, God moved upon government officials to grant Joe unprecedented permission to land wherever his ministry takes him. Joe takes a 360-degree pass over the strip to make sure the men of Santa Rosalillita have removed the rocks. They have. A dusty pick-up truck and three men are already waving from below, waiting to drive the team down the bluffs to their village.

Cuco, a village elder, ushers everyone into an abandoned, two-room structure that will serve as the clinic. The cinder-block cubicle is empty except for two wooden benches. Joe and Alma push them together and *voilá*, they have a pharmacy counter. They quickly unpack most of the duffel bags, arranging the medications in neatly organized rows. Joe switches roles (but never his beloved red baseball hat) and changes from pilot to pharmacist. Villagers are already clustering at the door, adding their names to a sign-in notepad. It's 9:30 and Dr. Avitia gathers his patients together to begin the day with a brief message and prayer.

By 2:30 p.m. everyone can feel the pangs of deferred lunch. Dr. Avitia insists he is not tired, just hungry! He has treated 38 patients, ministering to each one in the name of the Great Physician, explaining as he goes that he can treat symptoms but only God can heal. They must look to Him. Three of his patients asked for prayer today, wanting to receive Christ as their personal Savior. Many have already opened their hearts to Jesus on previous visits.

With just enough time to get back to the mission before dark,

"Flying for Jesus" takes off. 4,500 feet below, the crystalline sea reveals underwater tidepools visible even from the air. One incredible beach after another glides by, bays striped with perfect waves and trimmed in shimmering white sand. Hedged by rugged, trackless terrain, these beaches are as unattainable as a mirage. From the air, the desert is a beauty that flaunts her hidden treasures.

To the east, scrubby brown mesas rise from a wilderness creased by salty, dry riverbeds and deep arroyos. As the plane reaches the San Quintin valley, absolute desolation is replaced by a flatter patchwork quilt of cultivated fields. Still, the brown and tan shades of drought are only sporadically relieved by rare, precious squares of living green, as if the quiltmaker only had a few scraps to work with. Dirt roads stitch the patches together and, through it all, one satin ribbon of paved highway runs from Tijuana in the north to Cabo San Lucas at the southern tip of the peninsula.

The plane touches down once again, just outside Vicente Guerrero. Joe calls his wife Marian on the cell phone to let her know the team has returned safely.

Long ago a rich, young ruler in Palestine wanted to follow Jesus but faced one huge obstacle – his love of money and all that money could buy. In 1983 a rich, young real estate developer from San Diego began to struggle with the same dilemma. Joe Vaine had just encountered Christ and asked Him into his life. Little did he know what that would cost.

Joe's business talent had made him a multi-millionaire by the age of 38. He led a self-indulgent lifestyle that most men only taste vicariously through tabloids.

"But God knew just how to deal with me," Joe recalls. One week into his new Christian life, his girlfriend suggested they do a little cocaine. His protests were weak and easily overcome. Three days later, Joe discovered he had lost $50,000 in his business. A couple of weeks later, his girlfriend made the same suggestion. Joe complied. Three days later, he found he had lost $75,000. The third time they did cocaine, Joe lost $250,000, again finding out three days later. Finally, Joe prayed. "God, I may not be very smart, but I'm not stupid!" So ended the drugs, but not the love of money.

With money came pride. Wasn't God lucky to have Joe Vaine

on His team? Yessiree, Joe thought as he wrote out another check at church, he could really help God out.

Joe went through the motions of Christianity for several years, yet experienced only stunted growth in his spiritual wasteland. The fourth wife came and went. Joe sold his two homes and began to build his dream ranch in the gently rolling hills of Del Mar, California, overlooking the Pacific Ocean.

Still, beneath the veneer of success and pleasure, a hunger began to grow. Wasn't there more to being a Christian? More to experiencing the life of God? Joe began to attend week-night Bible studies at Horizon Christian Fellowship in San Diego. Suddenly, he began to devour God's Word like a starving man brought to a banquet table. For the next six years, he studied voraciously, attending Bible classes five nights a week.

Early in this season, God began to trouble Joe's heart about his "other god." He felt God saying to him, "I've given you much. What are you doing with what I've given you?" Unable to shake the nagging question, Joe decided to spend a day alone in the mountains seeking God and what He would have him do.

In truth, Joe didn't expect much to come of his scheduled appointment with God. Didn't things like this take time? Perhaps, he thought, after years of prayer and fasting, God might speak to him, allowing a little inspirational thought or two to come his way. For now however, Joe would pencil God into his daytimer for a brisk, Tuesday morning in January. No one could say he didn't give God a chance.

His silver and gray pick-up sat perched at the far edge of the highway turnout, high above the hazy expanse of the Laguna Mountains. Morning passed into afternoon. Joe sat in the driver's seat reading his Bible.

"You are going to fly for Me."

The voice spoke so clearly, Joe couldn't be sure if it had come from outside or within his own mind. He sat stunned and still. What just happened? Fear gripped him as he realized that his Creator, his God, had just spoken to him. The "big man around town" disappeared in one pounding heartbeat. Suddenly, he felt very, very small. Goosebumps covered his arms. In a flood of realization, Joe saw his own unworthiness before God and became painfully conscious of his sinful past. With a new humility, his shock turned to wonder. "Who am I, that God would even talk to me?" The experience was to remain a vivid and vital memory.

Joe flew down the mountain feeling nine feet off the ground, his spirit soaring with exhilaration. Still, he wondered what God meant. After all, he hadn't flown a plane in twelve years.

Being a businessman who was accustomed to making things happen, and happen quickly, Joe assumed that God – the Ultimate CEO – would be just as efficient. For about six months, he seemed to be right. Joe finished his instrument rating as a pilot. He found a used airplane in Texas, offered for sale by a fellow Christian. He explained to his business partners that God had called him to the mission field and began to phase himself out of the business.

Then a man invited Joe to fly with him on an outreach to Islas Marias, a prison island 100 miles west of Mazatlan. The trip went well and Joe returned heady with the thrill of evangelism and instant "success". Once again, the old pride crept into his heart. Boy, could he do a lot for God! He was a salesman by nature, full of persuasive talents. He even remarked to a friend, "This ministry stuff is a piece of cake!"

Today, Joe groans at the memory. "How I wish I could have taken those words back!" Joe recalls, "It seemed like all I could do after that was fail. I failed at everything."

The man in Texas turned out to be a fraud. Joe had sent $25,000 in cash based on a verbal agreement that the plane would be ready to pick up in 30 days. Fifteen months later, after interminable excuses, Joe drove to Texas only to find the man had been selling parts off the plane. Depressed and feeling like an idiot, Joe put what was left of the plane into his trailer and headed home with his "bucket of bolts."

He had the whole drive home to think about his attempt to do big things for God. His money, his efforts, his natural abilities – they had come to nothing. Back in San Diego, alone in the hangar at Gillespie Field, Joe fell prostrate on his face. "God, I'm sorry. I really messed up. Forgive me for taking advantage of Your grace, for thinking this was about me and what I can do instead of what You, in Your mercy, want to do in me."

About this time, Joe read the famous story of George Müller, a British man of faith who never spoke of his needs, but believed in looking solely to God to provide for the orphans in his care during the late 1800s. Suddenly Joe realized God was asking him to live the same way, in complete and sole dependence upon Him.

"What?" Joe argued. "I'm a good salesman. I can make money; I can raise money!" Humble pie is always hard to swallow. In Joe's case, it meant accepting the fact that God was not the least bit impressed with what Joe could do for Him. God only cared about what *He* could do through Joe.

In the silence, Joe knew. This was to be God's ministry, not his. That morning, Joe vowed to meet with God on the hangar floor each day at 8:00 a.m. "God," he prayed, "I'm waiting for You. I'm not going to make a move unless You provide."

One last idol remained – the house at the ranch. God was asking, "Me or the house?"

Joe recalls the inner turmoil. "I wanted to justify what I had. I could say, 'I worked hard for this; I deserve this' or be obedient to God's call." When Joe released the house, God gave him something in return – freedom. Freedom from the love of money and freedom from the pride of his possessions. God wanted Joe's undivided heart. Now He had it.

Marian, Mexico and ministry

The life of faith was nothing like life in business and it took getting used to! It's been said that a true Christian should live a life that makes no sense unless there is a God. For Joe, that meant walking away from calculated projections and five-year plans and simply obeying, even when he had no idea where the next step would lead.

Although Joe had no special interest in Mexico, a friend persuaded him to go down to San Quintin, Baja, to El Buen Pastor, a Christian clinic 200 miles south of the U.S. border. He went three times and met Dr. Alexandro Gonzales and his wife, Ruth. As they visited one afternoon, Joe heard himself sharing, "This sounds crazy but I think God is calling me to fly an air ambulance – free of charge." When he looked into Ruth's eyes, he saw tears.

"We've been praying for you to come for five years!" Ruth cried.

Ruth had no idea just how crazy the idea really was. He still had business obligations to disentangle from. And another detail – he didn't have a plane. What was God going to do?

True to George Müller's example, Joe never asked anyone for money or spoke of his need, yet over $30,000 came in over the next year to repair his remains of a plane. In addition, God sent several airplane mechanics who donated their labor. When Joe started to shop around for an attorney to form a non-profit corporation, the first man to step forward turned out to be a Christian who offered his services free of charge! From being "self-made" and proud of it, Joe was learning the delights of a "God-made" life, lived in trust and humble dependence.

Finally, Joe was ready to fly – solo. "Just you and me, God," he thought. After four marriages, he wanted to keep life simple. Then Joe met Marian.

Marian's own life had been scarred by two failed marriages and much personal turmoil. When her adult children invited her to attend Horizon Fellowship, she finally, and fully, surrendered her life to Jesus. Her son Garrett, challenged her to follow him in taking a nine-month course called "Lifestyle Evangelism". During that time she sensed God speak to her, "It's time to set your kids aside and let Me worry about them. Prepare yourself for missionary work."

Marian clung to Jeremiah 29:11, amazed that God still had any plan at all for her, considering what a mess she had already made of her life. Over and over, the Holy Spirit led her to verses that spoke of renewal and restoration. He would take all the pain and ugliness of her past and replace it with beauty. Marian no longer put any confidence in her own plans. She was now sure of only one thing; God had a grand adventure in store for her. As she puts it, "Nothing else mattered – being single, being 50, nothing – as long as I was in the center of God's will."

Shortly after graduating from the course, Marian joined the advance team for Horizon's Spring Festival of Life in Mazatlan. Night after night, she visited churches with the festival's promo film which showed Keith Green singing "People Need the Lord" in Spanish. Each night, she found herself bawling as she watched this song and realized God was calling her to Mexico. When a friend told her about Joe Vaine and invited her to join the prayer support team for Flying for Jesus, a fledgling missions outreach, she readily agreed.

When Joe met Marian Swanson, a woman at complete peace with being single, he felt safe. When Marian met Joe Vaine, a man described at church as having a 300-foot wall up against women, she felt safe. Here was a man as adamantly opposed to remarriage as she. What a comfortable relief!

But within months, both Joe and Marian, resisting all the way, realized God had united them in heart and vision. Once they sheepishly acknowledged this to each other, love flourished with a beauty and sanctity neither one had ever known in their previous relationships without Christ. Still, Joe questioned Marian, "Why would you ever want to marry someone like me? I'm selfish, set in my ways, and I'm a proven failure at this – four times over!"

Marian's answer stunned and silenced Joe. "Because you're a godly man."

Finally, Joe found his voice. "If I'm a godly man, it's only because of Jesus. I had nothing to do with it."

Joe and Marian had an unusual marriage ceremony. Before family members, they each recapped their lives and asked for forgiveness for any hurt caused by the way they had lived in the past.

After a year of marriage, the Vaines bought a mobile home near the airport in Santee, just east of San Diego, where Joe could spend his time working on the plane. These days brought more training in faith and dependence; when they left for Mexico in May of 1994, the Vaines had $50 in the Flying for Jesus account and one $50-per-month pledge of support.

Through the church at El Buen Pastor, the Vaines met Dr. Marco and Alma Angulo and soon discovered a common interest. Both Joe and Dr. Angulo shared a vision for medical outreach to people in outlying camps and remote villages. When the government gave approval for Joe to fly to these areas, both men recognized it as a miracle. God had opened the door.

When the Angulos joined the staff at FFHM's mission in Vicente Guerrero, Dr. Marco discovered others at the mission clinic and Bible school who shared the same vision. Soon Joe and Dr. Marco began flying with one or two nurses from the clinic each week to Calamajue, a fishing village just within round-trip fuel range. Eventually they began to take along Bible school students as part of their training in evangelism. Today, Dr. Ramon Avitia continues this outreach with Joe in a circuit expanded to six regular destinations.

As the ministry of Flying for Jesus seemed to naturally merge with that of the mission, Charla began to wonder if this could be the fulfillment of a vision given her in the 1970s. In this vision, God had showed her a turbine, its blades turned by a great wind that drove a ball of fire. The fire rolled from the mission down the peninsula. Did this mean the ministry of the Holy Spirit would someday go out from the mission to the remote areas? So far, their efforts had fallen far short of this vision. With Flying for Jesus, what once seemed impossible became an exciting reality.

In 2000, Charla and the board officially welcomed the Vaines and Flying for Jesus into the work of the mission. Joe, also a retired San Diego fireman, became the mission's official "fire chief," training other staff to assist in fire rescues and maintaining the fire truck and equipment. Today, the mission still provides the only fire service in the area and the only Jaws of Life rescue south of Ensenada.

Marian brings her valuable business skills to running the mission gift shop and overseeing the production of macadamia nut products. More importantly, she dedicates herself to covering the mission in intercessory prayer.

Back to the rich young ruler in Palestine. When Jesus asked him to sell all he had and give it to the poor, the man went away filled with sorrow because he just couldn't do it. Had he obeyed, he might have discovered how paltry his possessions really were in comparison to what Jesus was trying to give him.

One day the doctors at El Buen Pastor called Marian to the bedside of an American man badly injured in a motorcycle accident. Bandages covered his entire head, with the exception of one eye. His girlfriend, who lay in another room, suffered from severe, head-to-toe road burns and could not walk for the mummylike wrappings. A third member of the party, the man's friend, had escaped unharmed and waited nearby. Marian entered the room, expecting the meek response of a man needing help.

"Get my jet here to pick me up right now!" He issued orders

before Marian could even introduce herself. "And get me some-thing decent to eat. I'll pay whatever I have to."

Marian immediately called Joe in to deal with the patient's unreasonable demands. As hard as Joe tried to explain the circumstances, the man would simply not accept that money could not get him what he wanted. "Where do you think your jet is going to land?" Joe asked, slightly amused.

"In the city airport, of course," the man snapped.

"There is no city within a hundred miles. We have a short, dirt runway that can't possibly handle anything like that."

"Then fly me in your plane to San Diego. I'll pay you whatever you want."

Joe sighed. "You can't pay me for what we do."

"Yeah, sure. Look, whatever you want, I can pay it. You want big bucks, you got it." The man snapped his fingers at the nurse. "Bring me a phone!"

Joe continued, "If you want to go to San Diego, we'll take you there, but not for money. I'll do it because God cares about you."

Joe quietly left, handing Marian his cell phone. At the man's request, she called his secretary in Chicago. He ordered his private jet to be waiting for him just across the border at Brown Field in San Ysidro – with sushi on board.

During the flight to San Ysidro, the injured man grew increas-ingly agitated and grilled Joe about the ministry. Primarily, he wanted to know where the money came from.

"We never know. God just provides."

Joe's answers baffled him. They were beyond anything he could process. 1 Corinthians 2:14 says, *"The man without the Spirit does not accept the things that come from the Spirit of God, for they are foolishness to him ... "* Joe understood. Faith can look really stupid from the outside.

After landing at Brown Field, Joe taxied up to the waiting 50-passenger Gulf Stream, his little Cessna dwarfed by the sleek, corporate jet. The patient got on his plane, still trying to impress Joe with offers of big money.

As the Gulf Stream wheeled slowly for its take-off run, Joe prayed for the man inside. He thought of his own past when money had meant everything, yet had left him in profound poverty.

Beyond the airfield, a setting sun gilded the royal blue sky with splashes of gold, like a careless overflow from the treasures of a wildly generous king. Beyond the breathtaking expanse ... what? An invitation to eternity, a wedding feast, a mansion, the intimate company of God. Would the man eating sushi in his Gulf Stream ever know the true meaning of "rich"?

There is a love the Father freely lavishes upon His children – a love beyond anything we could ever earn or buy. The lover in Solomon's Song of Songs says, *"If one were to give all the wealth of his house for love, it would be utterly scorned"* (Song of Songs 8:7). Joe watched his old self fly away into the northern sky and contemplated how much his life had changed. If a selfish, arrogant developer from San Diego could learn about real wealth, there was hope for anyone!

"How priceless is your unfailing love!
Both high and low among men
find refuge in the shadow of your wings."
(Psalm 36:7)

PART V

Our Faithful God

In 1966, Charla's vision of a waving field of wheat in the desert seemed more like a preposterous hallucination. It was hard to imagine a less likely scene. Even in the spiritual sense, this was a barren wasteland – hardly a target population center for evangelism.

Yet, look around today! God has proven Himself completely faithful to that vision, to His Word, to His desire to save to the uttermost.

In this section, you will meet four children from the early days of the orphanage – Raquel, Angel, Araceli and Maria. These little ones have grown up, "oaks of righteousness, the planting of the Lord." Their stories are just a few of the many stories that could be told of God's faithfulness in bringing an awesome harvest to fruition.

"I planted the seed, Apollos watered it, but God made it grow.
So neither he who plants nor he who waters is anything,
but only God, who makes things grow."
(1 Corinthians 3:6–7)

Chapter 19

An Angel Gets His Wheels

"My soul will boast in the LORD;
let the afflicted hear and rejoice."
(Psalm 34:2)

Carlos slammed the door of the stolen Chevy Impala and pounded the dash with his fists. "Go! Go, man!" His rigid, adrenaline-charged body twitched and jerked like a short-circuiting robot. He threw an armful of beer six-packs and cigarettes into the back seat. "Get out of here!"

Puzzled, Angel revved the engine and the car spun around the corner, barely under control. When he finally stopped, Carlos yanked the door open and jumped from the car.

That night, Angel broke into a Good Year tire store for car parts. Everything seemed quiet enough. He pulled back onto the street. Suddenly the police were behind him. During his inter-rogation in jail, he found out why his friend had bolted in such panic. Carlos had killed the convenience store owner during the robbery. Angel was an accomplice to murder!

Many readers are familiar with Angel's early story from the first book, *Charla's Children*. Josefina Barajas, then a social worker from Ensenada, found Angel and his sister Rosa, at the dump and brought them to the orphanage which would later become the mission. Charla wrote, "Rosa, the seven-year-old, was one of the most pitiful sights I had ever seen ... Her four-year-old brother, Angel, crippled by polio and suffering from rickets and extreme malnutrition, was attached to her like a little monkey, his misshapen, bony arms and legs wrapped around her body."

Angel underwent eighteen surgeries at the Shriner's Hospital in Los Angeles between the ages of eight and sixteen, spending much of his childhood in body casts. By seventeen, his spine had been straightened enough for him to walk upright with the support of leg braces. A teenage sense of independence, new-found mobility and a curiosity to see the world converged. One day Angel slipped quietly out the door with nothing but a backpack and hitchhiked to Los Angeles, looking for the family of another boy who had grown up with him at the mission.

Alarmed for his safety, a staff member followed Angel and persuaded him to return. But a week later, Angel left again. This time, he got a taste of how bitter street life can be, sleeping under freeway bridges and working for food as he made his slow progress northward to the L.A. barrios.

A year later, Angel hitchhiked to San Jose and found work fixing cars for a man who ran illegal cock-fighting games. Restless and depressed, Angel stole his employer's car, pointed it south, drove until the gas ran out, then abandoned the car. He found himself back in L.A. embroiled in gang life.

Over the next few years, Angel spiraled down into a life of petty crime and drug use, going to jail many times and accumulating eighteen different aliases with the L.A.P.D. As he sees it now, the day finally came for God to stop his freefall in answer to the prayers of those who cared about him. Like Jonah, who spent three days in the belly of a fish coming to terms with his rebellion and God's will for his life, Angel spent the next three years in a California State Penitentiary.

Immediately upon parole, Angel returned to his brother Tony's house in Vicente Guerrero and soon gave his life back to Christ. A year later he married and settled in San Vicente, a town about an hour north of the mission. Angel managed well on crutches and found work painting cars for an auto body shop and making abalone jewelry to sell at the mission gift shop. Life resumed peacefully until 1997.

Angel never saw the drunk driver who hit him. Coming around one of Highway One's many tight turns, the large truck barreled straight into Angel's pick-up head on. The hood crumpled, giving way as the entire mass of engine and dashboard crashed down on Angel's knees, trapped under the steering wheel. Both knees shattered and Angel passed out from the pain. It took the ambulance crew two hours to extricate Angel from the twisted jaws of his mangled truck as traffic backed up for miles in either direction. With no anesthesia, the tortuous ride to Ensenada drove Angel in and out of consciousness. After surgery, Angel returned home but life was forever changed. Much of the mobility and freedom hard-won through years of childhood surgeries was lost in one moment of sickening impact. Now confined to a wheelchair, Angel wondered, "How will I support my family? How will I ever pay for the second surgery I need?" And the biggest question of all, "Why has God allowed this to happen to me?"

It never occurred to Angel to seek help from the mission, but Charla got word of the tragedy and immediately had Angel picked up and taken to the clinic in San Quintin for his second surgery. Even still, he struggled just to survive. Angel recalls this period, when it seemed like the accident had shattered his entire life. "That was when the blessing began," he muses.

One day Angel met one of the many visitors who come and go from the mission each week. Dirk Kos was a Dutchman from Canada. Dirk watched Angel struggling in a small, flimsy chair that barely moved on the rough terrain and tended to topple backwards whenever Angel tried to shift his large, husky frame.

"You know, Angel," Dirk said, "I'm pretty sure God brought me down here to Mexico to show me how to live for others, to care for others. Next month, you're going to have a new wheelchair."

Dirk Kos turned out to be an engineer who manufactured wheelchairs and prosthetics. "A genius," Angel insists. The chair arrived, cleverly customized to maneuver over rough ground with minimal effort.

This excited Angel, who had always been an inventive tinkerer himself. Dirk recognized a kindred spirit in Angel; here was a man gifted with the ability to envision what did not yet exist. Both men shared a great compassion for the physically handi-capped. Inspired by Dirk, Angel began to dream of putting his own mechanical ability and training to use in the Lord's service.

But once again Angel experienced the molding hand of God. The mission offered him a job, but it was nothing he imagined.

They wanted him to work in the kitchen! He hated the thought of mopping up after children, staff in "higher" positions, and often ungrateful guests. For a year, Angel did menial chores, chafing under this rub on his pride.

"When I ran away from here at 17," Angel admits, "I was a spoiled brat. Now God had to humble me. It was a wonderful, freeing moment," he recalls, "when I realized this is what Jesus did. He humbled Himself to serve others. I learned a lot here in the kitchen."

Angel also learned to pray. Specifically, he says, "I learned that prayer opens doors. I still longed to serve God with my hands, my mechanical ability, but it didn't seem possible."

Meanwhile, Dirk began to write to the Foundation board, sharing what he claimed to be a prophetic vision from God. "I know just one thing for sure, " he wrote, "that Christ is leading us . . . to provide for the handicapped a new lease on life through the mission in Vicente Guerrero." The board wrote back acknowledging the need but politely refusing. "We are already a multi-faceted ministry stretched to the limits," they explained. "We cannot consider adding yet another ministry at this time."

More letters came from Dirk and his wife, Mary. God had miraculously provided them with a large supply of donated wheelchairs through two major medical companies. In addition, their niece wrote from The Netherlands saying her college classmates had raised the equivalent of US $5,000. They wanted to send the funds to purchase the specialized tools and equipment needed to start a shop at the mission for reconstructing chairs and other devices. Dirk's conviction and persistence paid off. The board gave their blessing, a new ministry was born and Angel's prayers were answered.

Dirk recalls his shock and disappointment back when the board rejected his initial plan. "If we had gotten a 'yes,' we would have done everything our way. Instead, God took it out of our hands and opened His own doors." He laughs with delight at how God continues to miraculously provide. "We never wonder anymore, 'How are we going to do this? Or pay for this?' God comes up with His own solutions."

Angel agrees and shares one of many examples. Late in 2002, he met a paraplegic with a severe bed sore that had eaten three inches into his back. In addition to a chair, the man needed something called a roho dry-flotation cushion – rare, hard-to-get, and expensive. When Angel introduced himself, the man began to weep and said, "I just prayed for a wheelchair. I have to give this one back to the hospital."

Angel, who uses every opportunity to teach others to trust in God, prayed again with the man, urging him to look to his Heavenly Father for his every need. Together, they filled out a mission "needs request form". Even before they had a chance to turn it in, Angel found out the weekly truck with donations had arrived from the office in San Clemente. What was on the truck? A special tilting wheelchair with a roho dry-flotation cushion!

Since mid-2001, Angel has been working full-time in what is now called the "Angel Ministry", using his inventive, mechanical gifting to bless the many handicapped people in the area. In April of 2003, Angel built his own unique "hand-cycle" and completed the grueling, 50-mile Ensenada–Rosarito bike ride! The funds raised from Angel's sponsors will help him create and build more equipment for the needy and disabled of Baja.

Angel grins with obvious joy over his latest inventions. "Now I know why I am the way I am. God made me this way so He could use me. This has been the most wonderful year of my life!"

"For we are God's workmanship,
created in Christ Jesus to do good works,
which God prepared in advance for us to do."
(Ephesians 2:10)

Chapter 20

In His Arms

"He said to them, 'Let the little children come to me,
and do not hinder them, for the kingdom of God belongs to such
as these. I tell you the truth, anyone who will not receive
the kingdom of God like a little child will never enter it.'
And he took the children in his arms,
put his hands on them and blessed them."
(Mark 10:14–16)

Araceli

Tears streamed down nine-year-old Araceli's cheeks as her mother packed three of her siblings into the car, leaving her behind with two other sisters. She had been left at orphanages since the age of three, spending the last two years here in Vicente Guerrero. As the car pulled away in a cloud of dust, Araceli tried to understand this latest nightmare. Her mother didn't want her! Why else would she choose to keep the others, and not her? Anyone who listened carefully that day heard a little heart breaking.

For a few months, Araceli's mother came to visit her occasionally but the little girl refused to speak to her or even come out of hiding to see her. One day her mother asked, "Why won't you say hello or hug me?"

"I don't feel anything for you!" she screamed.

Her mother began to cry, fumbling through the shame and defeat she felt as she tried to explain herself. Araceli met her tears with stony silence. Soon after, her mother remarried and emigrated to the United States.

So many children like Araceli have either been left at the mission by parents who cannot care for them or have been taken from abusive parents and placed here by the state. Thankfully, God provided wonderful houseparents for Araceli through Antonio and Teresa Aguilar, a couple who loved and guided her during her most turbulent teen years.

When Antonio and Teresa left the house to be administrators of the Bible school, Araceli found it hard to deal with another painful loss. New houseparents arrived but Araceli grew resentful and rebellious.

The year she turned eighteen, Araceli accepted a marriage proposal . . . and heard from her mother. She would be visiting in two days! Hot tears poured down her cheeks as Araceli confided in her former houseparents.

"I don't want to see her! I don't want her to come to my wedding."

"Araceli," Antonio gently urged, "now is the time to forgive your mother."

"No!"

"You have accepted Christ and you need to obey Him," Teresa reminded her. "Change will only come when you ask the Lord to free you from your anger and give you grace to accept your mom."

Two days later, the bus arrived from town.

Araceli took one look at her mother and ran, only to be stopped by Antonio. He led her by the hand to her mother. She stood stiffly as her mother hugged her.

In the spring of 1990, Max Christian, the director at the mission, explained to Araceli that she needed her mother's consent to marry her beau, Manuel Hernandez. This posed another hurdle for Araceli's proud and hurting heart. She began to pray, asking God to change her and bring healing. Inwardly, Araceli knew Max was right in asking that she honor her mother and she felt God's peace as she agreed.

After the wedding, the couple moved into a small trailer provided by the mission and Manuel joined the staff, working in the orchard. About that time, Max Christian left and Corrine Ehrick accepted the director's position.

"Corrine taught me how to show affection," Araceli remembers. "Sometimes the kids here just don't get enough because the houseparents have so many kids to take care of. And so many come from abusive backgrounds. They grow up not used to being held and loved. Corrine always had a hug for me!"

Soon, Corrine asked Araceli and Manuel to serve as houseparents. At first, Araceli felt reluctant. Her first baby had just been born. Did God really want her to go back to an orphanage now that she finally had a real home of her own?

Cautiously, the couple agreed to help on a part-time, substitute basis. But Araceli soon realized this was where they belonged. God had uniquely equipped her to minister to these children. He had used people like Antonio, Teresa, Corrine Ehrick and others in her life. Now that cycle of love continued as she spent many nights just holding her children, encouraging them to talk, sharing with them the love of their Heavenly Father who would always be there for them. The couple's temporary commitment turned into ten years of anointed parenting as God brought many more little "Aracelis" into their lives.

In 1996, Araceli began to visit her mother in Los Angeles, California. On the third visit, the dam broke. Suddenly, at the breakfast table, her mother began to weep. "Araceli, you're my daughter. I've always loved you. Maybe I was wrong to put you in the orphanage, but I was trying to protect you. My husband was molesting your sister."

As her mother asked for forgiveness, Araceli held her and tried to comfort her. "God had a plan for me, Mom. He opened my eyes to a lot of things that I would never have learned if I was not at the orphanage. I met the Lord and I'm learning to serve Him."

Today, Araceli and her mother cherish a close relationship nurtured by a steady flow of letters and phone calls.

Manuel and Araceli now have three children and a home in town where Manuel works as a police officer. Araceli continues to serve on staff at the mission. She explains, "God showed me many things here – how to love people, how to forgive my mom and dad. God is using me here to talk to kids. I know how the kids feel and how much they need love, so I try to show them that love."

*"The L*ORD* is close to the broken-hearted*
and saves those who are crushed in spirit."
(Psalm 34:18)

Raquel

The skinny, eight-year-old girl shuffled her feet along the highway, creating little clouds of dust that rose into her trailing sister's face.

"Cut it out, Raquel!" Her sister closed the gap between them with a quick dash and smacked the younger girl on the shoulder. "Pick up your feet. You're getting my dress even dirtier."

Raquel grimaced. Who cared? They were just going to another orphanage, another ugly place with kids as dirty as they were. She hated them all. Another brother and sister toddled on ahead, each clinging to one of their mother's hands.

Raquel's mother cooked for highway workers. She followed them wherever the road led, making it impossible to raise her four children in any fixed location. Desperate to provide them a home, she had been going from one bleak orphanage to another, looking for a place she could bear to leave them. A friendly stranger mentioned one last possibility – Hogar Para Ninos Necesitados (Home for Needy Children), a mission in Vicente Guerrero.

Weary, hot, and pessimistic, the small troupe turned east off the highway for the last mile, squinting into the morning sun as they walked. Marta, the eldest daughter, picked up her little brother.

"Don't worry. Even if you stay here, mother and I will visit often."

"Why can't you stay, too?" he whimpered, his big, brown eyes welling up with tears.

"I have to work like Mama, you know that. Don't be afraid. I'm going to work in the packing plant just down the road. I'll be very close."

Suddenly, a bouncing bundle of dark curls, smiles and giggles hopped and skipped across their path. It was Estella, one of the mission children. Raquel's eyes grew big as she stared at the little girl's clean dress and polished shoes. With a newfound burst of energy, she caught up with her mother and tugged on her skirt.

"Mama! Mama! Did you see her? I want to stay here! I want a dress and shoes like that!"

For Raquel, the search was over. Later, in the office, she found out the children took baths and even got to go to school. She looked down at her rags and let her imagination run free. "Clean, smart, and a lady, that's what I'll be!" she dreamed.

"I'll stay here right now!" she blurted suddenly, growing impatient as her mother asked questions, answered questions and struggled to fill out paperwork.

Her mother smiled, almost crying with relief. Nothing could take away the pain of leaving her children behind, but at least they would be safe and welcome. Raquel's enthusiasm and independent spirit would help the younger ones adjust.

That first, warm bath felt like heaven to Raquel. Special soap killed the lice that had plagued her for so long. Many years later, as a grown woman, Raquel would remember the dress she received that day – green and white with a rounded, turn-down collar. She pranced about for days, tapping her new, patent leather shoes and admiring her lace-trimmed socks.

Raquel remembers, "I thought I was a princess doll, as beautiful as the rest of the girls. I took a napkin. Every time I thought about my shoes, I spit on my napkin and cleaned off the dirt."

Raquel had arrived mid-semester and to her dismay, the school would not let her enroll. Hannah, one of the mission volunteers, found her sulking over this disappointment.

"Tell you what, while you're waiting for the others to come home from school, I'll teach you to knit and sew," Hannah offered. By Raquel's ninth birthday, she had made her first dress.

Raquel soon caught on to the another wonder of life at the mission – peanut butter! Two big, plastic tubs were kept in the storeroom. One contained mustard, the other peanut butter. They sat in the same spot, mustard on the left, peanut butter on the right, day after day after week. Raquel figured out a way to carry a big spoon hidden behind her back. Whenever she had opportunity to walk by the storeroom, she would quickly dip her spoon into the peanut butter and run away, her mouth crammed with this sticky, stolen delight.

One day the director's wife, Kay Lawrence, caught her in the act but said nothing. Instead, she simply switched the position of the tubs and waited around the corner. Before long, Raquel arrived. Out came the spoon. Keeping her eyes on the doorway, the little girl dipped into the tub without looking at the contents. Her eyes still darting around, she popped the spoon into her wide open mouth. Kay pounced. One horrible half-second later, Raquel stood before Mama Kay; her eyes watering, throat burning, quickly forcing herself to swallow the most shocking, terrible stuff she had ever tasted! Kay still said nothing. Raquel smiled as naturally as anyone can while choking and keeping their lips pressed shut at the same time, then scurried away.

Raquel laughs at the vivid memory. "I never did it again, and I still **hate** mustard!"

Years later, when Raquel left the mission, Kay went with her to the bus stop. "Wait," Kay said, "I almost forgot to give you something." Kay turned around and Raquel knew she was crying. Kay finally handed her a gift – a Bible inscribed with her parting counsel, "Never depart from the way of the Lord."

Unfortunately, it took Raquel a few years on her own to learn the wisdom of Kay's words. In 1984, Raquel returned to visit at the mission in despair. She had married because of pregnancy and quickly divorced. Now, still a young woman, she was on her own with three children.

Juan and Elisa Carillo, houseparents at the mission for over twenty years, took Raquel into their embrace. They remembered Raquel as a spirited, young girl and rejoiced at her return. They showered her with the love she needed as she poured out her feelings of failure and guilt. Juan, a beloved father figure to so many kids at the mission, led her back to the grace and mercy of God.

Two years later, Raquel visited again – this time to counsel other young girls. She shares her mistakes openly and honestly. Kay's early words now come from Raquel with conviction, "Never depart from the way of the Lord."

Today, Raquel is remarried and lives in Sonora where she and her husband are both involved in their home church.

"My children love to hear my story repeated and repeated," she laughs. Recently, Raquel had a gift made for Charla that she brought from Sonora – an ironwood sculpture of a little girl nestled safely in the palm of Jesus' hand. Raquel explains, "I'm that girl because I met Jesus at an early age. I am in Jesus' hands, me and my whole household."

"I give them eternal life, and they shall never perish;
no-one can snatch them out of my hand."
(John 10:28)

Ana Laura

Fifteen-year-old Ana Laura sat at the kitchen table over a bowl of tortilla dough and listened with growing excitement. Her aunt, Tia Liduvina, had come all the way from the Baja to Morelia, in the center of mainland Mexico, to tell her family about Jesus. Tia Liduvina's words sounded so familiar. They triggered powerful memories of the orphanage in Vicente Guerrero where Ana Laura had spent much of her childhood. Ana Laura, Raquel's younger sister, had been taken from the orphanage at the age of ten and sent to live with her older sister, Irma.

Just hearing the name of Jesus once again thrilled her in a way she could not explain. Ana Laura continued her work, shaping the dough into guava-sized balls, then rolling the balls into thin, flat moons. Her sister, Irma, listened as well while keeping a watchful eye on the tortillas blistering on the hot pan. Tia Liduvina explained the gospel further and Ana Laura finally burst out, "I know about that! It's true!"

The next day, Tia Liduvina took the family to a church where Ana Laura gave her heart to Jesus. "I don't know if I ever did that at the orphanage when I was little," she says, "but I think that just hearing His name was the most important part of growing up there." Suddenly all the Bible stories and lessons from her early days were coming back with fresh meaning.

Three years later, Ana Laura graduated from Bible school and then spent several months in Acapulco with an American missionary couple. After returning to Morelia, Ana Laura experienced an intense touch from God and realized He was calling her to a ministry to orphans. Soon after, three different people shared the same scripture with her from Revelation 3:8, *"See, I have placed before you an open door that no-one can shut."*

"I realized," Ana Laura explains, "that this meant I didn't need to knock; I didn't need to wait for a key. I was just to step through the door in faith."

At that same time, another missionary couple, Lonnie and Darlene Inabet, asked an unexpected question, "Ana, when do we start building your church?"

Ana Laura laughed. "Me? I'm not a pastor!"

"Well, what *do* you want to do?" they persisted.

Ana Laura paused, then stated with absolute surety, "Lonnie, an orphanage."

Lonnie's eyes popped wide. "What?"

A few months later, the Inabets returned from their visit to Kentucky where they had spoken to their pastor and home church. "Ana, we need to start looking for property!"

Ana Laura was stunned enough at this "open door," but then it swung even wider. Irma, overhearing Lonnie's announcement, called from another room, "You don't need to look. I have a piece of property you can have." Irma had an inheritance she planned to split between her children and wanted to include Ana Laura. Knowing Ana Laura intended to use the property for an orphanage, she even gave her an extra share. For the next two-and-a-half years, teams came from Ohio and Kentucky until construction was completed.

One day, a letter arrived from the mission in Baja. Papa Juan Carillo, who had been a housefather there during Ana Laura's childhood, invited her to come for a visit and see old friends. On that visit, Ana Laura ran into Charla.

"Do you remember me?"

As soon as Ana Laura reminded Charla of her older sister Raquel, Charla laughed, "Oh yes, the one who gave me a few headaches!"

Somehow, as they struggled through Ana Laura's non-existent English and Charla's limited Spanish, Ana Laura told Charla about the orphanage in Morelia. She meant to ask for Charla's advice. Charla thought she was asking for "help" as in a formal, legal covering. Charla promised to meet with the board and pray about it. Ana Laura knew something had fallen into the language gap when, a few weeks later, Charla faxed Ana Laura agreeing to bring the Morelia orphanage under FFHM's umbrella.

"Of course!" Ana Laura immediately reacted, in spite of her surprise. "This is God!"

Suddenly, Ana Laura realized she wanted nothing more than to give the orphanage back to the Lord, by turning it over to FFHM. She explains, "My heart was so thankful. I had received so much, I wanted to give my all. The orphanage was my 'all.' Didn't God give me His all?"

For some time before this, the FFHM board had felt God calling them to expand the ministry but did not know where He wanted them to go. When they heard Charla's proposal, their reaction was identical to Ana Laura's, "This is God!"

Thus, Ana Laura's orphanage became the mission's new center in Morelia. In April of 2003, the center celebrated its fifth anniversary. The orphanage now has three housemothers who care for 31 children from Oaxaca whose parents are prison inmates. Every six months, the staff members take the children to Oaxaca to visit their incarcerated parents. When the center in Tlacalula is finished, these children will be permanently moved back to Oaxaca and the Morelia mission will take in new children referred by the local government. The center's church is flourishing and outreach to the community continues to expand.

Ana Laura, once a little girl who knew what it felt like to be separated from her mother and left at an orphanage, served as the center's gifted administrator for several years. She now serves on FFHM's board and continues to oversee the Morelia ministry. Think how many are blessed because of a little girl who fell in love with Jesus and wanted to give her all!

"How can I repay the LORD
for all his goodness to me?"
(Psalm 116:12)

Chapter 21

Set Apart

"I became a servant of this gospel by the gift of God's grace
given me through the working of his power."
(Ephesians 3:7)

The water in the irrigation duct flowed swiftly, sucked down the channel by powerful turbines at the pumping station a half-mile away. The duct cut through miles of tomato fields across the hot plains of Sinaloa. Eugenia, a single mother from Oaxaca, picked in these fields twelve hours a day. It was Sunday, her day off. Her three children played on the banks of the channel. Eugenia squatted by her tin bucket of laundry, pulled out a worn, faded shirt and slapped it onto a large rock. The sun blazed without mercy. She dabbed at her perspiration, trying to keep it from running into her eyes. She had to rest. Eugenia rocked back on her heels and lifted her head, trying to catch a breeze.

The air was too still, too quiet. Her baby son sprawled on a mat with one foot in the air. His big sister bent over him, pulling a sticker from his toe. One, two. Where was the middle one? Eugenia turned in every direction. No little two-year-old with a mop of black hair anywhere. Eugenia eyed the water with growing unease.

"Galia! Where's your sister?"

Galia dropped her brother's foot. "I don't know."

Eugenia shaded her eyes and squinted, trying desperately to see more, to see faster. She began to run along the bank, racing the current. Her scream carried back, "Look for your sister!"

There it was – a red mushroom of color bobbing in the tug and roll of the stream. Little Maria's dress! Eugenia flew, not feeling any of the sharp rocks and thorns that tore at her bare feet.

"Maria!"

The roar of the pump engines drowned out her own pounding heart. She wasn't going to make it. Run faster. The churning blades sucked at the stream, pulling Maria's body closer into their deadly embrace. She needed help. A desperate cry tore from the very center of her being.

"Jesus!"

Eugenia didn't even know who Jesus was. It was just a name she had heard. She knew and worshiped many gods, many spirits. Why, at this moment, had Jesus been the only name she could say? She would think about that later.

Seconds or minutes, it passed in a blur. Maria's limp body sagged in her mother's arms. Eugenia didn't know what happened. She could not remember going in after Maria, but here she was. Eugenia sobbed, sinking to the ground with the body still clasped tight. Water poured from the ears, mouth and nose; the stomach bulged with bloating. Her little girl was dead.

Eugenia thought again about that name she had cried out with such unconscious, gut instinct. Jesus. Why Jesus? Wrestling with a grief that strangled her words, Eugenia choked out a simple prayer. "Jesus, if You are real, give me my child back!"

An eternity passed in the next moments. Eugenia thumped on her daughter's back as if she could somehow loosen the grip of this monstrous death.

Maria's eyes opened.

"Mommy, why are you hitting me? I was already up there!"

Eugenia stared. Color poured back into Maria's face.

"Mommy, there was a man with white clothes. He told me I had to go back to my Mommy."

Eugenia knew nothing of the gospel but added the name "Jesus" to the list of saints and gods she prayed to. As Maria Villa Pablo grew up, her mother never tired of telling her the story of that incredible day. "Maria," she would say, "I know God saved you. Your life must have a very special purpose."

Eugenia's struggle to keep her family alive took her to the Baja Peninsula. Trudging to the work camps with two toddlers and a baby, she tried to find someone who would watch her children while she picked strawberries. Exhausted and on the verge of despair, she met someone with a rare bit of good news.

"Through those hills," the stooped, dark woman pointed, "there's a place. They take care of children." She directed Eugenia toward the tiny town of Vicente Guerrero.

Two weeks after coming to the mission, Eugenia's baby boy grew seriously ill. An amoebic infection in his blood had dehydrated his veins to the point of no possible recovery.

Leaving the hospital, Eugenia headed for her home, a tiny shack on the far side of the town dump. As she stumbled through the garbage and debris, she cried out once again to God. Suddenly, through the blur of her tears, Eugenia saw the fluttering of loose pages torn from a book. The fragile, white sheets seemed to jump out from the surrounding sea of plastic, rusting metal and ashes. Eugenia stooped down for the pages and began to read the words. They came from Genesis, chapter one. *"In the beginning, God created the heavens and the earth ... "*

Instantly, Eugenia sensed the excitement of an answer to a question she had always felt but never put into words – "Where did I come from?" Eager for more, she searched the ground around her. She turned and found an old book with a broken spine that had dropped its pages like a wintering tree. This was it! She read the cover ... Holy Bible ... and tucked it under her arm.

As Eugenia continued across the dump, two more items caught her eye. A statue of Jesus with a broken arm and a statue of the Virgin of Guadelupe. "Well," Eugenia thought, "I'll take them home and pray to all of them." Stopping at a small store, Eugenia bought three candles.

In the dark recess of her shack, Eugenia set up a mini-shrine with her three new treasures – two broken statues and an old, disintegrating Bible. A candle burned in front of each one as the desperate mother pleaded for the life of her son. She prayed until she fell asleep.

That night, Eugenia had a dream that changed her life. She saw the earth as a divided orb, half in darkness, half in light. On the dark side, she saw masses of people from every country and culture crying out to a countless variety of idol statues and images. They wept and begged, asking for every type of need. She saw herself among this pitiful throng, praying for her dying son.

Realizing the futility of her prayer, she decided to go the light side and ask for help. As soon as she took the first step toward the light, a voice called to her.

"Who are you?" Eugenia answered.

"Search the Scriptures, for they testify of Me." Gently, a pair of wounded hands placed a Bible into Eugenia's hands.

Still not seeing anyone, Eugenia called out, "What about my son?"

Suddenly Eugenia could see her son. The same hands that gave her the Bible were touching his face. Her son began to smile.

When Eugenia woke up, the salvaged Bible was in her hands, open to Matthew, chapter four. She read, *"Man shall not live by bread alone, but by every word that proceeds from the mouth of God."* She jumped up and raced to the clinic. If her son was well, she would know it was Jesus who had intervened in her life once again.

The doctors met her with amazed expressions. "We don't know when it happened, but it's miraculous. Your son is recovering!"

That day, Eugenia discarded all her trinkets and statues. "They belong to the dark side," she reasoned, remembering her dream. "They are just deaf idols who cannot answer or help me. Only Jesus has helped me."

After the children had been at the mission for eighteen months, a letter arrived from their grandmother in Oaxaca. She insisted the children be removed and brought to her.

The return to Oaxaca plunged the family back into the darkness of superstition and witchcraft. Grandma's constant warnings filled their young minds with endless fears. "Don't smile during the thunder; your tongue will fall out. Don't point at the rainbow; your hand will wither." On and on. Above all, they feared the evil spirit, Tabayuco.

The witch doctor came every month. Maria hated him. She hated his "cure". It was supposed to chase away the shadow of fear that hung over the children, but it only scared them more. The adults said Tabayuco came to frighten the people, especially the children. When you were afraid, your soul could be drawn away from you. In that state of soul-separation, any manner of evil could befall you – sickness, accidents, misfortune. Everything bad was blamed on Tabayuco. Tabayuco had to be driven away so they would not be so fearful, and thus their souls brought back to them.

Maria squatted with her back against the tree, wishing she could press herself into the moist, rain-soaked bark and disappear. Her grandmother yanked her hair and hissed at her to stay still. The other children watched, wide-eyed, as the witch doctor struck the clay bowl with a rhythmic beat. The tempo accelerated as he sank deeper into his trance state. A large boulder in the center of the clearing dripped with the blood of his sacrifice, Grandma's chicken. Most of the blood had been caught in another bowl and now the children were instructed to come forward. Maria felt like throwing up, crying, running away, all at the same time. Why did her mother bring her here? Her little seven-year-old body trembled as the witch doctor dipped his fingers into the blood, then touched it to her tongue, her ears and her knees. Lifting his head to the star-studded sky, he shouted out her name and the name of many other spirits, asking for their protection. Then his words became mysterious, garbled sounds that Maria could not understand.

That night, like so many others, Maria could see the evil spirits as their grotesque forms with bulging eyes manifested around her bed. When they jumped on her, she ran out into the darkness of the jungle, screaming, "You can't take me! I'm not going with you!"

During those early years, from ages four to eight, Maria knew she was not the only child living through this torment. But what could anyone do? These spirit beings were just a part of life. But for some reason, once a year, when her mother came to visit, the fear went away.

Those visits were wonderful! Eugenia told her children she was now something called a "Christian". She told them stories, sang to them, and prayed over them at night. They wanted her to stay with them forever. When Grandma died, Eugenia decided to return to Oaxaca for good. For a Christian, this was a dangerous decision.

Immediately, the villagers threatened to kill her if she did not stop talking about her strange beliefs. They said she was a traitor to their ancient religion. The children saw the hatred and cruelty inflicted on their mother and cried for her in secret. They lived with an alcoholic uncle who tried to kill Eugenia on many occasions.

Their Uncle Ramon beat the children and threw the females out of his house on repeated occasions. Once he sobered up, he would order them back again. Eugenia longed to flee but Ramon had one hold over her – her son. The uncle kept the boy close to him at all times and claimed him as his own.

One evening, Eugenia ordered her son to run into the cornfield and hide. Uncle Ramon drank heavily with his dinner. Eugenia waited until he fell asleep. Quickly, she gathered their few belongings and headed for the field.

"Lucia! Maria!" Eugenia whispered as loudly as she dared. "Find your brother and bring him to the road." She stood in the shadows, begging the clouds to cover the rising moon. If she could flag down a ride, they might make it to the city in time to catch a bus north. Three small figures appeared at her side, then crouched in the tall brambles. A pick-up driver saw the woman with her small bundle and swerved to a sudden stop. Eugenia cringed. The harsh screech of his brakes shattered the night and her nerves.

"Get in!" Four dark bodies crawled over the sides of the truck bed and huddled among sacks of coffee beans. Had Ramon woken up? Eugenia turned to look back towards the house and suddenly found herself staring into the beam of a flashlight. She froze in terror.

"You're not going anywhere with that boy."

Eugenia didn't need to see his face. She could hear the sneer. The circle of light danced around black lumps of burlap. Galia and Maria squirmed, trying to shove their little brother into a corner behind them.

"You stupid cow!" The beam had settled on two tiny feet poking out from Maria's skirt. Ramon's thick fist grabbed hold of the ankles.

The two sisters burst into tears. Eugenia tried to grab her son but Ramon's other fist slammed into her jaw and her head crashed against the tailgate. The driver didn't move, not wanting any part of this fight.

"Please!" Eugenia screamed. "He's my son. Let me have my son!"

The two girls joined her pleading, wailing in anguish as their uncle pulled the flailing, kicking boy from the truck. "You'll never leave with him," Ramon snarled. "If you come back, I'll kill you this time for sure."

Tears streamed from Eugenia's cheeks. She couldn't even hold him one more time. "I love you," she sobbed, reaching for her boy. "I'll come back for you. I promise."

Maria, her mother and sister arrived in Sinaloa, having traveled a road of heartbreak they would never forget. The last Maria heard of her little brother, he had run away to hide in the mountains.

In Sinaloa, the heavy work of a crop picker strained Maria's twelve-year-old body, especially her internal organs. Her mother decided to move to Baja where she heard the ranchers used smaller buckets for their tomatoes. And so it was that, after eight years' absence, Maria came to Vicente Guerrero once again.

The very first day after Maria's arrival, another young girl invited her to attend a children's Bible class to be held in the yard outside her home.

"If you come, you'll get a scoop of peanut butter and a glass of milk!" she told her. "Christians come from the mission in town. Sometimes they bring candy!"

The teacher was a young woman, a member of the outreach team from the mission – the same place Maria had been left by her mother when she was three years old. As the teacher began to tell the story of Jesus, Maria's heart jumped. Jesus! Why, He was the hero of her life! Other children had fantasies of Superman or Batman from the American comics, but Jesus had saved her from the aqueduct. Jesus had healed her brother at the point of death. Who could be more wonderful than Jesus? Maria strained to hear every word over the restless, noisy crowd. She wanted to know *everything* about Jesus!

As the other children busied themselves with crafts and games, Maria sat quietly on a rock, pondering what she had heard. The teacher noticed the shy, new girl and came over to talk.

"Why are you sitting alone?" the teacher asked.

Suddenly, Maria's story began to pour out in an unleashed flood of emotion. When she looked up, over one hundred children were crowding around her in absolute, rapt silence. The story ended and Maria began to sob uncontrollably with relief and joy. When the teacher asked if she wanted to ask Jesus into her heart, she answered without a second's hesitation.

"Of course! This is what I've been waiting for!"

Maria describes that day. "Something very special happened to me. From that day, I began to pray for my people back in Ucuji. I wanted to return immediately and tell them about Jesus."

For the next two years, Maria continued to work with her mother in the fields but spent every possible moment at the mission. She joined the discipleship class for girls taught by Graciella Cordoba.

Maria recounts, "Graciella taught me to walk with Jesus. I would say to myself, 'When I'm grown up, I want to be like her. I want to love God the way she does, to preach like she does. I want to know what she knows.'"

When Graciella invited Maria to eat in the mission dining hall, the sight astonished and thrilled her. Could there really be so many people in one place who loved Jesus? A profound sense of divine appointment enveloped her. She was home again!

At fourteen, Maria stirred up some controversy by applying to the Bible school. Wasn't she too young? Was she serious or just acting on adolescent emotions? After much prayer, the staff decided they simply had to recognize God's call on Maria's life and Maria became their youngest student.

Her class of five included Raul Garcia and Glen Almeraz. (Their stories are in Part I.) In hindsight, it seems obvious why Satan attacked the Bible school that year, completely destroying all the buildings in a freak flood. What enemy would want these fervent lovers of God to be equipped and trained to go out in the name of Jesus?

Two years passed and graduation approached. Two days before graduation, an invitation came for her to join a children's ministry team in Sinaloa. She had no money, no suitcase for her clothes; she had even lost her only Bible! Maria said nothing to anyone except God – "What now?" At the graduation ceremony, Maria received three gifts – suitcase, a Bible and exactly the amount of money she needed to go to Sinaloa. That day, Maria made a commitment. She would never hesitate to obey God, regardless of the circumstances.

After several months, a pastor invited her to come and work

with local churches in the lowlands of Juxtlahuaca, among the Mixteco Indians. It didn't matter to Maria that she was only sixteen and without family; she jumped at the chance to answer the first call on her heart – to return to her native people. It took three years however, for her to venture out from the ministry in Juxtlahuaca and ascend into the mountains of Ucuji, her home-land. The people there were still violently hostile to the gospel and filled with mistrust.

For the first year, Maria devoted herself to intercession for her people and waited for God to open doors. Those doors opened dramatically when a medical team visited from the mission in Baja. Maria recalls, "This really penetrated the walls between me and the people. They saw that I had not come to do them evil. They began to receive me in a new way and invited me into their homes."

As the walls of suspicion and fear came down, Maria began to form children's Bible clubs among the villagers and to teach adults to read and write. "In the past," Maria says, "this wouldn't have been possible. Before, they actually threatened to beat the children if they came to any of my classes."

Maria explains, "The people live in deep fear. They do not pray to their gods because they are good, but because they are afraid of angering them and being cursed by them if they do not."

Maria knew God was at work when a school principal invited her to teach a class on the basketball courts once a week before the start of school!

Maria continues to minister in this mountainous area six hours from FFHM's center in Tlacalula. Joy England from Glendora, California, faithfully worked alongside Maria for many years. In 2002, Maria's mother, Eugenia, and a younger sister returned to Oaxaca and now work with Maria! Galia, Maria's older sister, also graduated from the mission Bible school and is training to be a nurse.

Challenges abound in this remote area where missionaries are still stoned to death and villagers are brutally beaten for simply being friendly with known Christians. What encourages Maria the most? "To see thirsty hearts receiving His word. It doesn't matter what happens with my life, but only that those who have never heard the gospel will hear it at least once. God gives me opportunities wherever I go."

"I have one goal," Maria explains. "I want to bring joy to God's heart and to the hearts of others."

"Now get up and stand on your feet. I have appeared to you to appoint you as a servant and as a witness of what you have seen of me and what I will show you. I will rescue you from your own people and from the Gentiles. I am sending you to them to open their eyes and turn them from darkness to light, and from the power of Satan to God, so that they may receive forgiveness of sins and a place among those who are sanctified by faith in me."
(Acts 26:16–18)

Chapter 22

See His Glory!

As mere humans, do we not long to see God? To see beyond the veil that lies between the physical and spiritual, between the temporal and eternal? We have a gut yearning for our Creator, the One who gives us life and breath. Proof of this yearning is all around us in the myriad religions and spiritual disciplines of the world and history, all striving to lead man through the veil.

But who can grasp all that God is? Who can know an infinite Being? In this world, we are hopelessly limited in our experience of God because we have only a finite point of contact – our one life – brief in time, confined to a point in space. Mere mortals groping for the Immortal One.

We depend wholly upon God to descend into human affairs and reveal Himself to us. And He does! Do you long to encounter God in His glory? If so, you have something in common with Moses who pleaded for God's presence and then asked, "Show me Your glory." God granted him this request. Did Moses expect thunder and lightning? An earthquake or choirs of angels in blinding array to fill the sky? Celestial music or fire from heaven?

What was the glory of God? God answered Moses by saying, "I will cause all my *goodness* to pass in front of you . . ." Moses stood in the cleft of the rock and God covered Moses' face lest he die at the sight of God. Then God's glory passed by with the proclamation, *"The Lord, the Lord, the compassionate and gracious God, slow to anger, abounding in love and faithfulness . . . "* (Exodus 34:6).

This is God's own definition of His glory! When we experience His compassion, His forgiveness, His faithfulness, we are glimpsing His glory. When we receive His love and mercy, we are partaking of His glory. How did Moses react to seeing the goodness of the Lord? He fell down and worshiped. That is the natural and spontaneous response to any true glimpse of God.

God is not distant, hiding behind the clouds, silently leaving us to invent and speculate what He might be like. God wants us to know Him. He has revealed Himself to us. He has given us His Word, the Bible. He has sent His Son, Jesus Christ, who is also called the "Living Word." John 1:14 says, *"The Word became flesh and made his dwelling among us. We have seen his glory, the glory of the One and Only, who came from the Father, full of grace and truth."* Jesus came to reveal the true nature of God. Through Him, God's glory passed before us. He lived a life of compassion and mercy. He lived a life that did not condone evil, yet He offered forgiveness and grace. He delivered comfort and hope.

God continues to reveal Himself in many ways. He interacts; He intervenes; He speaks through His Word and by His Spirit; He lives through His people. Each story in this book illustrated an aspect of His character and nature revealed through His personal involvement in human affairs. I pray that, through these stories, *His glory* has passed before you.

If you have never known God, He is speaking to you through these witnesses. Each person in these stories would say to you from intimate experience, "He is altogether glorious and worthy of worship!"

If you are a Christian, you have been united with Christ and you share Christ's calling. By His Spirit who lives in you, you are called to live a life that glorifies God. In other words, your life mission is to live in such a way that the true nature of God is revealed. Will those who yearn to see His glory look at you and say, "Oh, *that's* what God is like?"

You've read the book. God has shown Himself to be the One who redeems the hopeless, who has compassion on the weak and suffering. He is sovereign in wisdom, all-sufficient to those who trust Him, and ever faithful. May you ponder what you have read and say, "That's what God is like!" And may your heart be filled with worship, for He is the Glorious and Worthy One.

Reader Contact Information

Would you like to know more about Foundation for His Ministry? They would love to hear from you.

U.S. Address:
Foundation for His Ministry
P.O. Box 74000
San Clemente, CA 92673-0134

Canadian Address:
Maranatha Evangelistic Association
P.O. Box 1292
Calgary, Alberta, Canada T2P 2L2

E-mail: info@ffhm.org
Website: www.ffhm.org

You may also contact FFHM to order your copy of *Charla's Children*. This 1987 Angel Award winner is Charla's own telling of the remarkable and miraculous early days of the ministry. Copies are available for US $10.00 plus $2.00 shipping.

If you have enjoyed this book and would like to help us to send a copy of it and many other titles to needy pastors in the **Third World**, please write for further information or send your gift to:

Sovereign World Trust
PO Box 777, Tonbridge
Kent TN11 0ZS
United Kingdom

or to the **'Sovereign World'** distributor in your country.

Visit our website at **www.sovereign-world.org** for a full range of Sovereign World books.